WITHDRAWN

COPING
WITH

Dating
Violence

Dating
Violence

Nancy N. Rue

THE ROSEN PUBLISHING GROUP, NEW YORK

Published in 1989 by The Rosen Publishing Group, Inc.
29 East 21st Street, New York, NY 10010

Copyright 1989 by Nancy N. Rue

First Edition

Manufactured in the United States of America

Library of Congress Cataloging-In-Publication Data

Rue, Nancy N.
  Coping with dating violence.
  Bibliography: p.
  Includes index.
  Summary: Examines the characteristics of abusive relationships and gives advice on how to get out of such relationships as well as how to avoid them in the first place.
  1. Relationship violence—United States.
  2. Acquaintance rape—United States.
  3. Teenage girls—United States—Crime against.
  4. Women college students—United States—
Crimes against.   [1. Relationship violence.
  2. Dating (Social customs)] I. Title.
HQ801.88.R84 1989 646.7'7 89-3459
ISBN 0-8239-0997-2

Manufactured in the United States of America

ABOUT THE AUTHOR ◇

Nancy Rue spent her first twenty-five years in the East. Born in New Jersey, she was raised in Florida, educated at Stetson University, DeLand, Florida (B.A., English) and the College of William and Mary, Williamsburg, Virginia (M.A., Education), and baptized by fire into a teaching career at Booker T. Washington High School in Norfolk, Virginia.

With her husband, Jim, she moved in 1978 to Nevada, where her daughter Marijean was born and where she taught for six years before "retiring" to free-lance writing. From the time she was ten, consuming two Nancy Drew books a day, she had thought she could write the sort of things kids could love. Now it was time to find out if she were right. With Fang, her computer, she has put out six books and more than fifty short stories, articles, and plays. Although awards have come her way (*Campus Life* Award of Merit and Outstanding Book of the Year award of the Books for Young Adults Program), she most treasures letters from readers who have consumed Nancy *Rue* books.

Along the way she and her husband became involved professionally in the theatre and together founded Nevada Children's Theatre. Their goal is to provide high-quality theatrical experiences for audiences of—you guessed it— young people.

Contents

COPING
WITH

Dating
Violence

CHAPTER 1

Kathi and Gary's Story

athi at fifteen was what used to be called a "P.K."—
Preacher's Kid. Brought up in the sheltering arms
of the church, she knew of almost nothing but
parish suppers and Bible study groups. Yet she was never
one to accept it all unquestioningly. Snapping her black
eyes and tossing her thick mass of dark brown hair, she
argued with her father's theology, challenged her mother's
edicts, and generally bristled under the constraints of
being a minister's daughter, making it known that that
wasn't all she was.

What she *mostly* was, people said, was boy-crazy. When
other girls were still dressing their Barbie dolls, Kathi was
following Little Leaguers around, finding out what made
them tick and what would make them pay attention to her.

From the moment she found *out* what made them tick,
she always had a boyfriend. Not one to play the field, she
was strictly a one-man woman, and although her current
man may have stayed her good graces only for two or three

weeks, she was devoted to him during his term. When the sparkle wore off, she was never unattached for long. Almost before she had time to scratch out one guy's name on her notebook, another's was being lovingly inscribed.

Until Gary came along. Kathi knew as soon as she won him over that she wasn't going to let him go.

Two years older than she, Gary oozed self-confidence. He seemed to know how to handle every situation, and he certainly knew how to handle Kathi. Flowers, stuffed animals with "Wuv You" embroidered on them, and cards with "God loves you and so do I," written in his inimitable hand—that hooked her.

Gary was the son of devout fundamentalist Christians who had raised him according to strict principles. These had had a positive effect on Gary, who didn't swear, smoke, drink, do drugs, or pursue premarital sex. He was what his friends called "totally straight." Yet his squeaky-clean reputation didn't render him obnoxious. He was well liked by everyone, probably because he was outgoing, sure of himself, and always moving toward a goal. With everything well in hand, he made people feel secure when he was around. He definitely made Kathi feel that way.

She submitted willingly when he decided that her little outbursts of defiance had to go. There would be no more bad language. Okay, said Kathi. No more irreverence. Her father deserved her respect, and so did his church. Okay, said Kathi. And she would have to clean up her act. She had too much class to be acting like a fool. Okay, said Kathi.

Her parents were amazed at the calming effect Gary seemed to have on her, and while they were slightly concerned at the dogmatic turn her opinions suddenly seemed to take, they decided she could go through a lot worse "phases." What no one seemed to see, least of all

Kathi, was that she was so eager to please her tall, sandy-haired, honey-voiced Gary that she was willing to undergo a personality transplant.

It wasn't surprising that Gary was able to pull off such a feat. They were together at every conceivable moment. Gary picked her up in the morning and drove her to school, where they sat in his pick-up truck until the first bell rang. He walked her to class and reminded her to wait there for him when first hour was over. That was the routine until lunchtime, when they took the lunch Kathi packed for them out to Gary's truck and ate together. After their two afternoon classes, they went to Kathi's house and did their homework until it was time for Gary to report for work at the local miniature golf course.

In the evening, Kathi was to wait for his phone calls. At the end of his last call, Gary always said, "I want my voice to be the last one you hear before you go to sleep," at which point Kathi would hang up and go directly to her room—to dream of Gary, of course.

When Kathi turned sixteen, Gary got her a job at the golf course so they could spend *more* time together. Picking up trash, cleaning johns, and fending off smart-mouthed sixth graders who complained about "trick holes" made it something less than a glamour gig, but Kathi found out that if she flashed her pixie-like grin at people, especially the males, they smiled back and subsequently gave her less flack. But it was a method Gary didn't like. Their first real argument was over the fact that Kathi said more than a friendly "Enjoy your game," to a college freshman she waited on. "I don't want to see you flirting with guys," he told her. "It makes you look cheap."

His demands prickled between Kathi's shoulder blades, but she gave them her best shot. If he was that jealous, it must mean he really loved her, she thought.

It was shortly after that when Gary's world began to fall apart. Already under pressure from his father to make up his mind what he was going to do with his life after graduation, he was jolted even further from his complacency by his parents' announcement that they were filing for divorce.

Gary was angry, terrified, confused. The jolt to his deeply ingrained moral standards was overwhelming. What happened to the marriage vows made before God? What happened to family being the top priority? And worst of all, what would happen to him? First they were forcing him to make decisions about adult life he wasn't ready to make, and now they were telling him there wouldn't be a family to back him up. An oppressive sense of loneliness descended on him that even Kathi couldn't fill.

That was largely, of course, because he wouldn't let her. For the first time he realized that his unusually mature poise was little more than a facade. When it came right down to the nitty gritty, he was as vulnerable as anyone else. But he didn't dare admit it. He'd lose his reputation, he was sure, and his status, and his self-esteem—and definitely Kathi. She'd see him for who he really was, and he couldn't have that.

Determined to stay on top of things, Gary tightened up. He was angry most of the time and took out his rage on the walls of the golf hut or the tires of his car. Kathi was frightened by the way each new confrontation with his father sent Gary into a frenzy. Once he smashed the side of his truck with a wrench. Another time he hurled his books across her living room. But never did she dream that the boom might some day be lowered on her.

One evening while Gary was patrolling the course and Kathi was at the counter taking tickets, two of her old boyfriends stopped by. They chatted for a few minutes, and then one of them offered Kathi a sip out of his cup. With her usual spontaneity she said, "Sure", and to her surprise gulped down a mouthful of beer.

The two boys hooted as she coughed and gagged and swatted at them, all the while laughing herself. But out of the corner of her eye she spotted Gary, who had spotted *her* having too much fun with someone else. Shooing her two accomplices away from the counter, she dug into her purse for a breath mint and had just crammed a handful of Sweet Tarts into her mouth when Gary was beside her.

She tried to smile coyly up at him, but her lips froze. The look on his face went beyond grim, or even angry. There was pure hate in his eyes.

Grabbing her by the arm, he steered her past the door marked "Employees Only" and slammed it behind him. He accused her of drinking. She denied it. He squeezed her cheeks together roughly with one hand and ordered her to spit out whatever she had in her mouth. She did and hung her head, waiting for the lecture. It didn't come. Instead, he picked her up by both arms and shoved her against the wall.

The shock hit both of them instantly. Staring at him in disbelief, Kathi began to sob. Gary's throat tightened and his face contorted to keep his own tears back.

The apologies were immediate and profuse. Gary swore he'd never hurt her again and begged her to forgive him and give him another chance. And he meant it. Without Kathi, he felt he just couldn't go on.

Clutching her bruised shoulder Kathi continued to cry, but she wanted to believe him. He stayed wth her until she tearfully agree to forgive him.

In the next two weeks Gary's behavior assured her that he would keep his promise. He showered her with presents and poems and attention—almost ad nauseam. It seemed only reasonable to assume that he had merely cracked under the pressure in his life and that he would never do it again.

But three weeks later he punched her in the arm when she "got out of line." And several days after that he pushed her, several times, hard, against the trash cans in her back-yard until she was crying hysterically. A week or so later he grabbed her so tightly that he left five fingerlike bruises on each arm.

The assaults got worse. Gary would storm into her house to pick her up in the morning for school, still seething after a fight with his father or an emotional scene with his mother. Hardly looking at Kathi, barely realizing she had even spoken to him, he would twist her first words into an excuse to hit. There would be a breath-stopping punch in the stomach or a sharp slap across the chest or a shaking that made her brain slosh against her skull.

Each time the abuse was more severe and the time since the previous attack shorter. Yet there was never an incident when Gary didn't break down into immediate remorse, smother Kathi with apologies, and plead with her to let him try just once more to get a handle on his rage. He would appeal to her sympathy for all he was going through, remind her of how much he cared for her, of how much he had tried to do for her.

Where was Kathi coming from during these months of hell?

She was trying with everything in her to understand what was going wrong. Her concern for Gary and the pain he was suffering at home was real, and she hated to do anything to upset him more. But the holding back of her own anger and righteous indignation was tenuous at best. During periods of peace she found herself playing the role of shrew, picking at him, criticizing him, getting his goat because she had no other way to express her frustration. When he erupted in a fit of rage, she retreated into guilt. *She* was making him hit her, she decided. It was her fault. He was going through a tough time. Why couldn't she be more understanding? Why couldn't she give him a break? It seemed as if he were another person when he was hitting. He didn't even look like Gary when he clenched his teeth and came after her. It was probably something he couldn't help. He was completely out of control. It wasn't Gary she was beginning to hate, she decided. It was that other person.

One morning when she was putting on a long-sleeved blouse on a 90-degree day to hide the large bruises on her arm, she thought how fortunate it was that he never hit her in the face where bruises and welts would be hard to conceal.

And then she stopped cold. Was it just luck that he had never slapped her across the mouth or broken her jaw? Or was he being *careful* not to leave marks that could be seen? With a sinking feeling she realized that Gary knew exactly what he was doing.

Kathi immediately went on an all-out campaign to avoid fighting with him. She stopped yelling back and arguing. She gave in before discussions got heated. She could tell when he was going to come after her by the way he slammed his belongings around, called her names, and broke, smashed, or threw the nearest inanimate object. When she saw it coming she talked soothingly to him and said she was sorry, even if she hadn't done anything even worth arguing about. Whereas for a time she had taken to returning his punches blow for blow, now she froze and did nothing to fan the fire.

But the abuse continued, and the reality of her situation crept in. If she wasn't the cause of it, she would not be able to stop it. She had no control at all. If she stayed and allowed the situation to worsen on its present course, she would end up maimed. There was no way to fix it.

Several months had elapsed since the first time Gary had hurt her. In all that time, while she rammed around in a panic, she never went to anyone for help.

In the first place, she didn't think anyone would believe her. Gary was so well accepted and popular that she was sure anyone she told would think she was either exaggerating or out-and-out lying. She had always been the rebellious, uncontrolled one, not Gary.

She also felt too much shame to share her predicament with anyone else. Her self-confidence was at an all-time low; she couldn't think of anything except what a mess she had made of things. It was hard to say that her boyfriend was beating her up when all her friends seemed to have such perfect romances going for them and when everyone was saying how good Gary was for her.

Kathi toyed with the idea of confiding in her parents, but she had never been particularly comfortable talking with her too-busy father, and she was rightly worried that her mother would forbid her to see Gary anymore. As much as he was hurting her, she cared about him. She wasn't ready to let go.

So it went on, Gary hitting Kathi harder and more often, Kathi staying and taking it; Gary believing he had no control unless he was hitting, Kathi believing she was a failure unless she could somehow stop it; both of them fighting to hang on—until the night Gary let fly with a punch that rendered Kathi unconscious.

I'm telling you about Kathi and Gary not because they're unusual and shocking, but because what happened to them is *typical* of what's going down with many dating teenagers today. We don't hear much about it because girls like Kathi aren't telling. But it's happening.

Here's what the experts estimate:

- According to Jean Doss, former public education director for the Committee to Aid Abused Women (CAAW) in Reno, Nevada, one fifth to one third of all teenagers who are involved in dating relationships are regularly abusing or being abused by their partners verbally, mentally, emotionally, sexually, and/or physically.[1]
- *Twelve percent* of the high school students surveyed in an Oregon study in 1982 reported experiencing abuse in their dating relationships, from age fifteen on, a statistic that has been confirmed by subsequent studies. That's one out of every eight.[2]
- In a study conducted by researchers at California State University, Sacramento, 27 percent of the 256 seventeen- and eighteen-year-olds questioned had been involved in violent relationships. Adding *threats* of violence as a characteristic brought the figure up to 35 percent. Yet only a small number of them felt it was a reason to end the relationship. One fourth even saw it as an act of love.[3]
- Lisa Morrell, intern for the Center for Women's Policy Studies, says that researchers assert that premarital violence occurs with approximately the same frequency as marital violence—between 30 and 50 percent.[4]
- Claudette McShane, in an article on date abuse in the November 1985 issue of *Campus Life* magazine, says that date abuse occurs in as many as 50 percent of all relationships.[5]

That means that as many as half of all young people who are building partnerships, learning the skills they'll later take into marriage, are pushing, shoving, hitting, kicking, choking, and threatening with weapons the very people they claim to love.

They're saying, "*I* love you, but nobody else ever will." They're hurling insults like, "You f-ing bitch. You aren't shit!"

Boys are isolating girlfriends from all other friendships with fits of jealous rage. They're tying girls up to keep them from going out while they themselves cruise Main with their friends or do a shift behind the counter at Burger King.

And they're forcing unwanted sexual contact—from an undesired kiss to an uncomfortable touch to actual rape. As many as one third of all rapes committed in the United States each year, writes Elizabeth Rodgers, contributing editor to *Seventeen* magazine, are committed by a girl's own date, boyfriend, or fiancé.[6] In fact, the peak age for acquaintance rape is sixteen for boys, fourteen for girls.[7]

In short, the very idea of love in the minds of 50 percent of dating teens could be turning into a nightmare—forever.

If the statistics aren't convincing enough, the kids involved are.

"You see girls in the locker room with welts on their arms," says Laurel, a fifteen-year-old whose former boyfriend threw her against a motor home and punched her in the stomach. "You know they came from their boyfriends, because you've seen their boyfriends slapping them across the face and pushing them against the wall, right in the halls at school."

Katie, a sixteen-year-old victim of an abusive relationship, says, "It happens a lot more than you know. Until I started confiding in a few of my friends, I didn't realize it was happening to them, too, and to their friends, A guy gets serious, a girl doesn't want to make a commitment, she tries to leave—and he hits her. He gets drunk or he's on drugs—and he gets violent. He gets jealous—and he goes berserk. I tell you, it's happening."

Even boys who aren't involved in date abuse admit to its occurrence in their own circles. As Scott, a fifteen-year-old sophomore, so bluntly put it: "He wants to have sex. She won't do it, so he beats her up. Then probably about half the time he rapes her, too."

People who work with teens are also seeing the evidence. "Today's boys don't seem to realize that today's girls don't take orders too well," says a high school counselor. "The boy starts making demands, the aggressive girl tells him to knock it off, and pretty soon they're duking it out right here on campus. It's a very scary problem. I'm frightened for our kids."

Private health care professionals come in contact with the problem as well. Merry Severance of Severance and Associates in Carson City, Nevada, explains that although most young people don't come to her with date abuse as the presenting problem, many reveal it as part of the reason for their depression. "For some of them, that boyfriend or girlfriend is their only reason for living—or so they think. Then when the boyfriend puts them down and pushes them around, or the boyfriend himself feels he can't control his aggression toward his girl, it can really get tough emotionally."

If this kind of violence is happening so frequently, why isn't it common knowledge? For several reasons:

- Girls like Kathi are afraid to talk about it, afraid they won't be believed, afraid they'll get the abuser into trouble, afraid they'll be looked down on, afraid they'll be forbidden to see their boyfriends again.

- Boys like Gary are terrified to go for help, afraid they'll get into serious trouble, afraid they'll be dubbed "crazy" and "put away somewhere," convinced they'll be prohibited from seeing their girl-friends again.
- Many adults don't take teenage romance very seriously in the first place. How could a relationship between people so young get that intense? It isn't possible, they say.
- Society as a whole often tends to ignore the things about itself that are less than pleasant. That applies to dating violence just as it once applied to domestic violence—and in many cases still does.

But the truth is that what happens in teen dating is *important*. The sharing, the laughing, the gentle touching, the aching together through each other's hurts aren't empty activities. They are the things that shape future relationships. They are the building blocks for marriage.

So, unfortunately, are hitting and browbeating and name-calling if they occur in the steady-dating scene. "Abuse during the dating relationship," writes Claudette McShane, "is a virtual guarantee of later abuse." If a couple for whom abuse is the norm decide to marry, they're in for a lifetime of battering that could leave one or both of them dead. One survey of battered wives at a shelter in Detroit revealed that 29 percent had been abused by their husbands before they were married.[8]

Even if a violent couple don't marry, the scars and tendencies carry over into future relationships if nothing happens to change them. In his extensive study *Violent Men*, Hans Toch reports that the probability of violence in personal encounters increases with each new act of aggression. If a person discovers that he can satisfy new and unsuspected needs by becoming aggressive, he'll continue to meet such situations by lashing out.[9] If a boy has learned to "solve" romantic problems by hitting his girlfriend, he'll hit his wife as well. And if you don't believe that "many" husbands are beating their wives, take a good hard look at the undeniable statistics.

- According to Federal Bureau of Justice statistics, 4.1 million cases of family violence occurred between 1972 and 1981.[10]
- In a study done in New Castle County, Delaware, Dr. Steinmetz found that 60 percent of randomly selected couples had engaged in some form of violent physical behavior during their marriage, and 10 percent of those admitted that the abuse had been extreme. Using the 10 percent figure, that's 4.7 million badly battered wives in the United States today.[11]
- Sociologist Richard Gelles's landmark study at the University of Rhode Island showed 55 percent of the couples engaging in one or more violent acts of spouse assault, 21 percent regularly, meaning anywhere from six times a year to daily.[12]
- Between 200,000 and 800,000 battered wives seek divorces every year, few if any after one isolated assault.[13]
- Statistics estimate that a woman is battered by a husband or boyfriend every eighteen seconds in the United States. Every year more than one million need medical help. Every day four die.[14] Thirty percent of all female homicide victims are killed by

their husbands or boyfriends, and, says the FBI, a history of battering accounts for 25 percent of all suicide attempts by women.[15]

- According to a 1983 report from the Attorney General, battery by a husband or boyfriend is the primary major cause of injury to women—more than rape by strangers, mugging, and car accident.[16]
- Raymond Parnas's study *The Police Response to the Domestic Disturbance* concluded that more police calls involve family conflict than do calls for all other criminal incidents, including murder, rape, non-family assault, robbery, and mugging combined. Wife-beating is three times as frequent as rape.[17]
- A report prepared by the National League of Cities and the United States Conference of Mayors sums it up: "The incidence of wife assault is so pervasive in this society that half of all wives will experience some form of spouse-inflicted violence during their marriage, regardless of race or socioeconomic status."[18]

If you already have a fifty-fifty chance of being injured, maimed, killed, or, at best, humiliated in your future marriage just by virtue of the numbers, then for those for whom "romantic" violence is already the norm it seems inevitable. James Koval, a therapist who counsels violent unmarried couples, says, "The roots of marriage are not in the ceremony and the honeymoon but in the dating period."[19]

What does that mean for you as a dating or about-to-be-dating teenager?

- It means you need to know what an abusive relationship is.

- It means you need to know how to stay out of one.
- It means you need to know how to get out if you're already in one.
- It means you may need to change some of the things you believe that could lead you right into a harmful marriage someday.

It's probably safe to say that you don't want to live in a society where violence of any kind is accepted as the norm, as a viable option for solving problems or releasing tensions or expressing feelings. Unfortunately, right now it is. You can take a step to change that. You can start with your own life. You can read this book and take it to heart.

CHAPTER 2

What Is Abuse?

E ric and Julie are in the school library working on a project for a class. It goes great until Julie's boyfriend Keith arrives, catches what he views as a "cozy little scene," and skips simmer on his way to boil. He rams through several people waiting in line to check out books, slams his fist on the table where Eric and Julie are doing research, and says to Julie in a voice loud enough to be heard down at the gym, "You *slut!* What the hell is this? I can't trust you for a minute!" Eric protests that he and Julie are doing an assignment, but Keith cuts him off as he jerks Julie out of her seat by the arm and practically drags her out of the library. Once in the hall, a terrified Julie says, "Okay, Keith, if you don't want me to talk to Eric anymore, I won't. I'll get Mrs. Anderson to assign me another partner." Keith feels better, tells Julie he's sorry he got a "little upset"—and everything's all right.

Right?

Wrong! Keith and Julie couldn't be further from "all right." They're in the beginning stages of an abusive relationship, and if Keith chooses to continue to use violence and Julie chooses to stay with him, they're both going to be in real trouble.

Yet chances are that you see this kind of thing going on from time to time, and you may not realize that it's something more than two people involved in a "stormy" romance. It's important to know that situations like Julie and Keith's can be called a number of different things— violence, abuse, or battering—but they all spell danger. If you date at all, or plan to date sometime in the future, or know people who date, it's important for you to understand what *abuse* in a relationship is.

Conflict occurs in every relationship. No two people can spend any amount of time together without disagreeing on *something,* even if it's just what toppings to order for their pizza. Those differences can be dealt with in a variety of ways, including arguing about the issue (into eternity!), folding your arms and giving each other the silent treatment, and storming out of the Pizza Hut and hitching a ride home. Not all of those reactions are going to solve anything, nor are they terribly pleasant, but they aren't violent or abusive. They won't cause either party physical injury or long-term mental anguish.

But when the inevitable conflict causes acts of aggression that are designed to hurt, control, and dominate another person, that isn't just "fighting" and disagreeing. That's battering. That's abuse. That's violence. There's a difference, and you need to know that difference so you will never accept abuse—in yourself or in anyone else.

Let's spell out the definitions carefully.

Abuse is the intentional use of physical, verbal, or emotional force or attack to control and maintain power over another person by frightening and intimidating her.[1]

A battered woman is one who is the victim of repeated physical or emotional abuse or both by her husband, ex- husband, boyfriend, or lover who is jealous and control-

ling and uses threats and verbal abuse as well physical violence to dominate her.[2]

A violent relationship is one in which the abuse of a partner becomes more frequent and more severe over time.

Every relationship is different, and if it's a violent one, its pattern of violence will probably be different from those of other violent relationships. But certain qualities are common to all abusive steadies. It's important to be able to recognize them.

1. A layer of gentleness often masks an abuser's potential to be brutal. The girl is usually surprised the first time he blows because he "seemed so nice at first," and so she tends to blame herself for bringing out the worst in him.
2. The incidents of violence are unpredictable. It's impossible to tell when they're coming.
3. The abuser is usually overwhelmingly jealous, not only of other guys but of the girl's family, friends, and anything that takes time away from him.
4. The abuser tends to conceal his handiwork, seldom hitting his girlfriend in the face unless the attack is particularly severe.
5. Alcohol is often involved, though not always.
6. Psychological abuse usually precedes the physical abuse. Name-calling, destruction of prized possessions, constant put-downs are not uncommon in violent relationships.
7. The abuser has to be in charge of the relationship, and his girlfriend believes that he is.

Our definitions and symptoms have so far implied that in a violent relationship the boy is the abuser and the girl is the victim. The first question most people ask when they hear that is, "Hey! What about girls being abusive to guys? I've known some pretty nasty girls! It happens, you know!"

Yes, it does happen, and everything this book says about the *abuser* applies to the girl who batters physically and emotionally just as it does to the boy. For the most part, however, what you'll read here is directed to the male abuser, and for several reasons:

1. Abuse of girls by boyfriends happens more often than the reverse. Boys grow up thinking they have to take the lead and are more likely than girls to use violence to do so. The injury of a boy by a girlfriend is an isolated case, and though it needs to be dealt with, it doesn't constitute a large-scale problem. The chances of a girl's being attacked or forced by a male date are far greater than the chances of a boy's being maimed by a girl he's dating.

2. A boy is usually more capable of inflicting real physical injury on a girl than vice versa. The occasional lady wrestler notwithstanding, let's face it: When a girl slaps her boyfriend across the face she leaves a stinging red mark and a certain amount of humiliation; when a boy hauls off and smacks his girlfriend in the face, he's very likely to leave a bruise, damage an eye, snap off a tooth or two, or even break her jaw. A boy has more density, more weight, probably more muscle strength, and, ten to one, more practice. He's hitting a body that in all probability is lighter, smaller, and more vulnerable than his. It isn't okay, mind you, for a girl to slap a boy. That isn't the way to handle the situation, and it's still a violent reaction. But because we're talking about a pattern of abuse that

can harm people physically and emotionally for life, it makes sense to hone in on where the worst of the problem lies—with the guys.

3. Yes, a woman can do just as much damage with a weapon as a man, and many women have been known to kill their husbands with guns. But teen violence rarely comes to that, and the women who break out the pistols, rifles, and shotguns are often those who have been repeatedly battered and see no other way out of their misery. It's just that sort of thing we want to stop by showing you what is okay and what's not from the very beginning of a relationship.

So as you continue to read try not to get caught up in gender. Think about *people,* not *guys* or *girls.* We have a *people* problem here. One *person* is abusing another *person.* We need to put an end to it. Let's start by being more specific about just what constitutes abuse.

Emotional Abuse

When you think of battering, you might immediately think of black eyes and bloody noses, and in part you're right. But a violent relationship usually begins to *be* violent with the use of emotional abuse. Even if emotional battering is used without physical violence ever entering in, it's still abuse. It's still dangerous to the health of the victim.

Violence is any behavior that causes fear in another person, and emotional abuse is certainly a violation of another person's psychic peace. A person who receives any of the following kinds of treatment in a relationship is emotionally abused:

- threats of physical violence, verbal as well as through shaking fists, sudden movements, a menacing look in the eyes, or a cruel tone of voice;
- unjust and continual accusations (of having an affair with someone else, of flirting with other people);
- public humiliation;
- derogatory name-calling and use of obscenity;
- continual ignoring or denial of one's feelings, thoughts, or needs in the relationship;
- constant criticism and verbal put-downs (It's your fault, You're a failure, You're fat, ugly, or sexually undesirable);
- forced isolation from family and friends;
- abandonment in dangerous places;
- destruction of valued property or cruelty to pets;
- betrayal of intimacy (laughing at expressions of affection, discussing and putting down certain sexual behavior in front of other people—"You kiss like a frog." "You don't know how to turn a guy on").

Those behaviors are abusive simply because they can destroy one of a person's most valuable assets—her self-esteem. If a girl begins to believe what that kind of treatment tells her, she learns to hate herself and is no longer able to do anything to help herself. Chances are that if the couple continue to see each other, verbal and mental abuse will escalate to physical abuse.

A close look at the list shows that there are really two ways to use emotional violence. One is the direct and obvious approach. If someone is recklessly driving the car you're riding in, careening around corners on two wheels and darting in and out of traffic at ninety miles an hour, it's terrifying because your life is in danger and degrading because the driver has so little regard for your safety.

If someone pelts your entire collection of cassette tapes against the wall or deliberately rips your favorite necklace off you and grinds it to a pulp with his heel, it's a violation of you as much as of your property. It's humiliating and maddening, as well as frightening. As you watch the plastic shatter or the silver twist, you may imagine yourself in place of the object, and understandably so. If a person can smash something that belongs to you without so much as a by-your-leave, he can just as easily do it to you.

Even merely yelling obscene words is a form of psychic violence because it does damage to the victim's self-esteem. If you're regularly called "bitch," "slut," or "whore" in a voice designed to slice through you, you are not going to feel terribly good about yourself no matter who you are! And once those words start firing through the air, the physical violence they excite can easily flare up, too.

The other form of emotional abuse is harder to recognize because when it's happening it doesn't seem like violence at all. It's called *social battering*—the extreme possessiveness that cuts a girl off from everything in her life that doesn't involve her boyfriend. When a relationship like this begins, the girl might actually enjoy the fact that her boyfriend wants her with him as much as possible, and she might even be touched when he pouts because she's spending the night with a girlfriend or going shopping with her mother. But before she realizes it she's dropping out of clubs and activities, drifting away from her friends, even studying less because he's taking over her life. He intrudes on her every thought and action, telling her what to wear, whom to talk to, how to act in the halls at school. Because he has manipulated her into believing that she's a mess without him, she really thinks she can't make a decision or form an opinion on her own. She may also find herself avoiding social situations because she's tired of defending his outbursts or because she's afraid he will start jealously accusing her of something in public and embarrass her beyond belief. He, on the other hand, might refuse to go to parties or on double dates because that's the only time she'll express her anger at *him,* since she's pretty sure he won't hit her in front of other people. It's the *hostage syndrome* in action. Her every move is monitored and controlled. She's completely dependent on him. And she doesn't even know how it happened.

Even physical abuse itself doesn't merely inflict bodily harm. In fact, the greater damage is usually mental. Every time a girl is punched or slapped or kicked, her self-esteem goes down the tubes a little further. She starts to believe that she deserves it or it wouldn't be happening. She becomes exhausted and scared and thus can't do anything to stop the violence. She becomes helpless and hopeless, a state that transfers to everything else in her life. She's a bundle of shame and self-hatred and stuffed-away anger. That's no way for anyone to feel.

So physical abuse *is* emotional abuse, even if it's just hanging over the victim's head. If a girl becomes comletely passive and submissive to avoid being grabbed and thrown against the wall, she's still being abused. She has exchanged her right to make decisions and express herself for not being physically assaulted. That's the result of violence. That's abuse. That's battering.

Physical Abuse

Physical abuse is the use of physical force or attack to control and maintain power over another person by frightening and intimidating her. Acts of physical violence can

be looked at on a scale from minor to severe. Minor physical abuse includes:

- a "playful" punch, done intentionally, that hurts,
- a session of excessive tickling that goes on even after
  she asks seriously that it stop,
- a pinch on the arm,
- a smack on the rear,
- a yank on a handful of hair,
- a slap in the face.

As physical violence slides toward the more severe end
of the scale, it includes:

- punching,
- kicking,
- biting,
- stomping,
- severe shaking,
- throwing dangerous objects with the intent to
  connect,
- twisting or breaking arms,
- pushing or throwing across a room or down stairs,
- burning from irons, cigarettes, coffee,
- choking,
- beating,
- stabbing,
- shooting.

The results of these extreme forms of violence include
broken bones, severe burns, concussions, permanent brain
injuries, hearing or sight loss, and sometimes death. But
even if the injuries are not visible or severe—even if a girl
comes out with an armful of bruises or the threat that next

time he's going to rearrange her face—it's still battering and it's still dangerous. If violence occurs more than once in a relationship, it's likely to occur again, and violence always becomes *more* severe, never less so. What today is only a scratch may tomorrow be a broken nose. Perhaps just as important is the intention behind an act of violence. Is it violence if a boy grabs his girlfriend by the wrist to make her go with him when she doesn't want to go? Yes, because he's using physical force to make a person do something against her will. No matter how minor it seems, that's violence. That's abuse. That's battering.

Sexual Abuse

A person's first dignity is her right over her own body. If she feels dread, fear, shock, horror, humiliation, disgust, or even just reluctance over anything another person is trying to make her do with her body, she is being sexually assaulted.[3]

The idea that date rape is the only form of sexual abuse in a relationship needs some rethinking. Sex that causes a person to feel hurt or degraded or worthless or ashamed should never happen. Anything connected with sex that brings out those feelings is abuse. Let's look at some examples:

- A boy who simply will not take no for an answer when a girl is sincerely saying, "I don't want to." "You're just saying no because girls are supposed to say no," he says, and keeps pushing.
- A boy who threatens as a means of forcing a girl into sex. "If you won't have sex with me I'll tell everybody you did anyway." "I'll go after your sister." "I'll leave you."

- A boy who uses insults to get his way sexually. "You're a whore." "You're frigid." "You think you're too good."
- A boy who uses manipulation. "If you love me, you'll do it." "Don't you like me?" "Everyone does it." "You're not afraid of me, are you?" "If you won't let me, I'll hurt myself."
- A boy who uses physical force or threat of physical harm to force a girl to participate in any sexual behavior, whether it's kissing, intercourse, or a form of intimacy she just doesn't like.
- A boy who rapes.

Although, again, rape is not the only form of sexual abuse that occurs in young relationships, it's a good idea to take a closer look at it. What actually constitutes rape is the use of force. The problem when it happens with a couple who know each other is that it may not seem like force at all at first. It may seem more like "bargaining," where words are used instead of physical force at first. Other factors may cloud the issue for you, too, so let's clarify. Forced sexual intercourse is rape even if:

- you know the guy;
- you've dated for a long time;
- you have let him touch you in intimate ways;
- you are drunk;
- you've had sex with him before;
- you give in out of fear, confusion, or guilt.[4]

Some people make a distinction between "sexual exploitation" (taking advantage of or manipulating a person into sexual activities) and "rape" (physically, violently forcing sexual activity). But the only real difference is in how much and what kind of force is used. So when Pammie at age fourteen was picked out by one of her brother's seventeen-year-old friends at a party, plied with wine, talked into going into a bedroom, and frightened into having sex on the bed, she was raped—even though she never said a word, even though there wasn't a mark on her, even though she felt that somehow it was her own fault. Somebody had dominated her, making her afraid to do what she wanted and say what she thought. That's abuse.

When you're involved in a violent relationship with someone you really care about, it's sometimes very difficult to see that your relationship *is* abusive. None of us likes to admit that something in which we've invested so much of ourselves is bad for us. The shame and humiliation in facing the fact that the boy you love is battering you is sometimes just as bad as the battering itself. For the good of both parties, though, it has to be faced. If you even remotely suspect that your relationship with someone may be abusive, try taking this quiz. If you answer yes to more than half of the questions, you are a victim of woman-battering. Please remember, it isn't your fault. You are in no way to blame for what's happening to you. Your only responsibility is to save yourself from it.

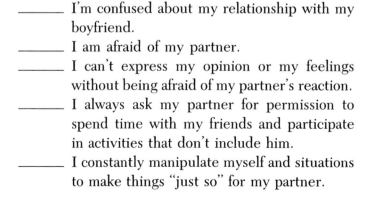

_____ I'm confused about my relationship with my boyfriend.

_____ I am afraid of my partner.

_____ I can't express my opinion or my feelings without being afraid of my partner's reaction.

_____ I always ask my partner for permission to spend time with my friends and participate in activities that don't include him.

_____ I constantly manipulate myself and situations to make things "just so" for my partner.

_____ I try and try to please my partner, only to be criticized again.

_____ I feel that my boyfriend is trying to run my life.

_____ I'm beginning to believe all the terrible things my partner says about me and accuses me of. Sometimes I'm not sure what's real anymore.

_____ Our relationship feels out of control.

_____ My friends have advised me to drop him.[5]

Whether you have been or are now being abused by a boyfriend, you are a boy who abuses, or you have a friend who's involved in a violent relationship, you need to remember three things even if you don't remember anything else we've discussed in this chapter.

1. Violence is an unhealthy, dangerous way of dealing with the anger, stress, and frustration that occur in any relationship.
2. It can have serious physical and psychological consequences in the end, no matter how minor it may seem now.
3. Abuse is against the right of every human being to have his or her body respected. It's also against the law.

It's abuse. It's violence. It's battering. It's bad stuff. To stop it, we have to change our attitudes about some things. Let's find out what those are.

CHAPTER 3

Destroying the
Myths

Since the first time a person looked up at the sun and wondered why it acted the way it did, myths have been used to explain things people haven't understood. Myths have made it easier to deal with the mysteries of everything from thunderstorms to where babies come from.

But a myth becomes dangerous when it covers up the truth about an important issue—an issue such as violence between people who claim to love each other. Many of the myths that are widely accepted in our society about men, women, and their relationships keep woman-battering alive. Before we can begin to put an end to violence, we have to take a look at some of the beliefs that we blindly nod our heads to but that simply aren't true.

Myths About Relationships

Myth: In a perfect, fairy-tale romance, the strong boy

29

takes care of his fragile girlfriend. He should therefore be in control of the relationship.

Fact: In the first place, there is no such thing as a "perfect, fairy-tale romance," but when you're weaned on "Cinderella," "Sleeping Beauty," and "Snow White and the Seven Dwarfs" it's no wonder you grow up believing that men are active, dominant, aggressive, and responsible for rescuing women, who are passive, submissive, helpless, and incapable of protecting themselves. When you believe that, you're also likely to believe that it's okay for a man to beat up his woman when she gets out of line because, after all, he's in charge and she's subject to that authority.

Those expectations put a great deal of pressure on a boy who, because he's a human being, doesn't feel strong, capable, and in control twenty-four hours a day. If he has to keep playing the role of the fairy-tale hero when in actuality he's feeling weak and insecure and vulnerable (the way a teenage boy probably feels about 80 percent of the time!), he often blows and starts swinging.

Myth: Okay, so if the boy isn't in charge, the girl is. After all, *somebody* has to control the relationship.

Fact: Human relationships are not power-centered, one-way affairs. Of course, people don't live happily ever after. Stress and conflict and change have to be dealt with whenever two people team up. But the best relationships are those in which a couple work together to solve their problems and settle their differences. Sometimes the boy feels more confident than his girlfriend and can say, "Let's try it this way." At other times it's the girl who takes the situation in hand. It just isn't healthy for either one to be totally in control—ever. If that happens, force is part of the relationship, and when you have force, you have abuse.

Myth: Love is when two people are so crazy about each other that they can't stand to be apart.

Fact: No, that's addiction. If he's possessive and jealous, he doesn't love her. He only needs her to inflate his ego and give him power. Sort of a holdover from the cave days. Real love is when two people want to be together but have times when they need to be with other people, get involved in other activities, and have some space.

It's when a relationship becomes obsessive—when people think they can't live without each other—that the danger of abuse creeps in. If a guy feels that he'll die if his girlfriend leaves him, he may do just about anything to make her stay. If a girl thinks she'll die if the relationship breaks up, she'll endure just about anything to keep it alive.

Myth: There are times when it's perfectly understandable for a man to slap his woman. Some situations just call for it.

Fact: According to one study, one fifth of all Americans still believe that.[1] Some of those are even wives who think their husbands should smack them on appropriate occasions, "for their own good." But there are no "appropriate occasions." No one has the right to hurt another person physically, emotionally, or sexually for any reason. Nor does it ever do anyone any "good." The abused person is probably scarred emotionally and possibly injured physically, and the abuser grows deeper into the habit of using violence to solve his problems instead of discovering ways that will make *him* a happier person. Besides all that, the male in a relationship is not a father disciplining a child. It's not his job to decide what is for his girlfriend's "own good." She's his equal. She can and should decide that for herself.

Myth: A boy is justified in forcing a girl to have sex with him if she has flirted with him or led him on but then refused to go further.

Fact: In a study by the National Center for Prevention and Control of Rape conducted with teenagers in southern California, over half the boys said they felt this was true—and almost half the girls felt the same.[2] But although sexual teasing doesn't show a whole lot of respect for another person's feelings, it isn't grounds for rape, and forcing a girl to have sex is rape no matter how you look at it. Yes, a girl ought to decide beforehand how far she's going to go and make that clear to her date. But if for some reason she doesn't, her date still has no grounds for forcing her to do anything she doesn't want to do. If he tells her she's a tease and he never wants to see her again and takes her home and leaves her stunned on her front doorstep, that's okay. If he tells her by God she's going to do it anyway and then rapes her, that's not okay. That's violence. That's abuse. That's against the law.

Myth: It's okay to hit a girl if she hits you, too.

Fact: Unless she is defending herself, a girl shouldn't hit her boyfriend because he says or does something she doesn't like, any more than a guy should start swinging. But even if she hits him and it's not in self-defense, that doesn't give a boy the right to hit her back. No one should accept being hit. But the way to deal with being hit is not to strike back, but to walk away from the situation and make it clear in a nonabusive, nonphysical way that you will not accept being hit.

Myths About Girls

Myth: A girl's highest goal is to catch and keep a man.

Fact: If you ask a teenage girl what she wants in life, she may say say she wants a husband, a home, and a family, and there's nothing wrong with that as long as her *highest* goal is still to be fulfilled as her own person. The danger in believing that any other person is your reason for living is that you'll put up with anything to keep him there and make it work. If "anything" includes abuse, you're in real danger of losing yourself entirely.

Myth: The female is responsible for making the relationship work.

Fact: Because traditionally the woman has stayed at home and taken care of the house and put the meals on the table and made everything wonderful for her man when he came home, it has been natural for people to assume that it was her duty to keep their interactions as a couple smooth-running, too. After all, he worked all day and is tired; she had better figure out some way to make his home life serene. Unfortunately, that has been miscontrued even further so that some people believe that if the man is unhappy, it's his woman's fault, and if he's unhappy enough to hit her, she must have done something bad enough to make him do it. Again, if a woman decides to be a full-time homemaker, fine. But it is neither all her job nor all her partner's job to make their relationship work. It's something they do together. If either of them is unhappy, they need to sit down as a team and work it out. Never, under any circumstances, does either of them have the right to slug the other. Unhappiness doesn't justify violence. Nothing justifies violence.

Myth: Some women deserve to be hit.

Fact: All of us have moments when we aren't exactly saints, and nothing brings those moments out like a love relationship. But none of us deserves to be bitten, slapped, kicked, humiliated, or demoralized for our less-than-saintly moments. We may deserve to be told that this relationship is over as of now. We may deserve to be taken home, hung up on, or dropped off at the nearest phone booth with a quarter, but none of us deserves a punch in the mouth— for anything.

Myth: Some girls actively provoke beatings.

Fact: No amount of wheedling, whining, cursing, or flirting with some other guy across the table is justifiable provocation for violence. Girls are not beaten because they ask for it. They are beaten because their boyfriends *choose* to use violence to deal with a situation. That doesn't mean that it's okay for a girl to do whatever she wants in a relationship. A boy has a perfect right to tell his girlfriend he doesn't like what she's doing, to tell her he's taking her home, to tell her he's out of there for good. He doesn't have the right to use any kind of emotional, physical, or sexual force because he thinks she's asking for it. Why in the world would she ask for it? When a girl verbally or mentally pushes a guy who's already on the brink of a flare-up—something you may have witnessed—she's often doing it in a desperate attempt to exercise some control over her life. Later, when she's nursing a bloody nose, she like everyone else may believe she provoked the attack. In reality, her assaulter could have chosen to storm out and slam the door. Instead he chose to hit her. That's abuse. That's violence. That's battering.

Myth: Some girls enjoy being hit. That's why they stay and put up with it.

Fact: Professionals who work daily with battered women will tell you that no woman wants or likes to be beaten. If you think about it carefully, you'll realize how ridiculous the myth is. You may like to play football, but do you like to have your ribs broken, your tendons pulled, your ankles sprained as a result? Of course not. That's absurd. You might risk having those things happen because you love to play, but the injuries are not what you like about the game. It's the same with violent relationships. Girls may stay in them for a number of reasons—including fear, helplessness, or the things they want or appreciate in the relationship—but their love of broken bones, black eyes, and public humiliation isn't one of them. They're emotionally dependent and afraid, possibly, yes. But masochistic, stupid, or weak? Definitely not.

Myth: Girls never like sex, so they have to be pushed into it.

Fact: Although a girl's sex drive may not have reached its peak at age sixteen the way her boyfriend's seems to have, that doesn't mean, one, that she doesn't enjoy sex, or, two, that she deserves any kind of force to get her into bed. She is a sexual being. She has complete control over what she does with her sexuality. No one has the right to make those decisions for her—verbally, mentally, emotionally, or physically.

Myth: A girl owes a boy sex, because—

Fact: Forget the becauses. No person owes any other person anything sexually for any reason. A guy spends $500 dollars on a corsage, a limo, and a seven-course dinner on prom night? You owe him your thanks, not your body. A girl bakes you brownies, does your chemistry homework, bails you out of jail? You owe her a thank you, not a sexual commitment. If there's no owing, there's no forcing to collect on your debts.

Myths: Girls always say no to sex, but with those tight jeans and all you can tell they don't mean it. Pushing for sex is just part of the game.

Fact: First of all, if sex is being played like a game, that's bad news. If a girl says no, the guy needs to believe her, period. If the girl has been using no to make the situation more interesting, she'll try another tactic. If she's been saying no because she means it, the guy will have shown her the respect she deserves as a human being. Period. Whether no means no or it turns out to mean maybe, no forcing is allowed!

Myth: Only minority or poor women are abused.

Fact: Violence in male-female relationships knows no barriers. In one study comparing the number of cases of domestic violence in a New York ghetto to the number in an upper middle-class New England suburb of the same population, virtually no difference was shown. If you are a white girl living in a two-story house with two cars in the garage, you are not automatically protected from coming up against a date who chooses to use abuse to solve his problems and get control over his life and yours. You need to know as much about dating violence as your black, Mexican, or American Indian friend.

Myths About Guys

Myth: A boy can't help it when he hits a girl. It's just uncontrollable rage.

Fact: If he was out of control when he slammed her against the wall, why didn't he pick up a knife, too? Rage is not uncontrollable. When any person chooses to harm someone physically, he does just that—he *chooses*, not out of loss of control but as a way of getting control. He knows what he's doing; evidence of that is in the fact that so many men who batter are careful not to hit in the face. "Rage," says one counselor, "wouldn't be so careful not to leave facial bruises."[3]

Myth: Alcohol and drug abuse causes boys to be violent.

Fact: Studies show that 25 percent of men who abuse don't use alcohol at all, and another 25 percent batter whether they're drinking or not. The correlation with drug use is even less.[4] Being drunk or strung out may make a guy more likely to choose to use violence, but the choice is still his. Look at it this way: If you ran over a child and killed him while driving drunk, would you say to the judge, "I couldn't help it—I was drunk"?

Myth: Guys who abuse are mentally ill.

Fact: Studies show that there is no more incidence of mental illness among woman-batterers than there is among the general population.[5] Saying that a guy is just "sick" eliminates the responsibility and keeps him (and the rest of us!) from having to confront the attitudes, beliefs, and institutions that have traditionally made it okay for a man to hit a woman.

Myth: Boys always want sex no matter what.

Fact: Boys don't "always" want sex any more than girls "always" want sex. If a girl believes that, she might also believe that if she doesn't give in when a boy pushes for a love-making session, she's somehow torturing him—the old "Baby, you've got me so excited there's no way I can stop now" myth. As a result, force is allowed to happen, and it's allowed to work! There is no physical reason why a guy has to have sex because he's aroused. He may feel frustrated, but he isn't going to die.

Some of these myths are so much a part of our thinking as a society that it's naive to think we'll eradicate any of them with the simple statement: "That's not true." But if we can replace them with other ideas that *are* true, maybe we can take a step toward understanding and eliminating violence in relationships.

These are the basics that refute any myth you can name connected with relationship abuse:

1. It is the *abuser's* behavior that provokes and continues violence, not the victim's.
2. No one has the right to physically, emotionally, or sexually force another person in a relationship. *Nothing* justifies violence.
3. The use of violence is a *choice*. Everyone gets angry, but there are ways to be angry without abusing.

If you are dating or plan to date in the future, knowing and believing these basics can help you to see your way clear out of a violent relationship should one happen to you. Learn them. Live them. In the long run, they could save your life.

CHAPTER 4

Why Boys Abuse

Tony punched Suzanne in the stomach because she wouldn't kiss him in front of a bunch of people. Chris hurled Laurel against a motor home because she broke up with him, even after he "changed his whole life" just for her. Jesse locked Paula in a walk-in closet before going off to play in a basketball game because he didn't want her flirting with guys in the stands the way she always did.

At least, those were the reasons Tony, Chris, and Jesse gave for those particular instances of abuse, but the real causes for lashing out in such violent ways go much farther back and really have nothing to do with the situation at hand. If flirting with another guy were a real cause for violence, would there be a dating girl in America without a black eye?

The choice to respond with violence isn't the result of anything anyone else does to a guy. It's the result of a complicated web of mistaken beliefs and hurts and anxieties inside *him* that even he probably doesn't understand. But it's important for him and the people around him to try to know what's going on in there, *not* to justify what he's doing—because nothing justifies violence—but for these reasons:

1. *If you're a batterer:* to make you realize that you need help to stop your hitting habit; to show you that you're not an uncontrollable, mentally ill monster and that you *can* change.
2. *If you're afraid you might become a batterer:* to help you take a look at the things you need to work on to avoid it.
3. *If you're battered girl:* to give you the reassurance that it's nothing you are doing that's making your boyfriend abuse you; to make you realize that *you* can't change him.
4. *If you date or plan to date in the future:* to provide you with information that can keep you out of a violent relationship.

The first thing to remember about a boy who uses violence is that he does so by choice. Although he may seem to be completely out of control when he barrels in with fists flying, he knows what he's doing. He could have walked away. Instead, he started whaling.

But *why* do some guys make that selection? Again, it's complex, but talks with woman-battering men and boys have revealed a number of basic reasons that work in different combinations in different guys to produce angry young men who think they have to hit.

Reason #1: It works!

A sharp slap in the face to your "opponent" can sure put a quick end to an argument, and most guys who choose violence as an alternative in a conflict have trouble talking things out and communicating in any way other than rolling up their sleeves. The slap, the punch, the spit, the obscene lanugage produces the desired result: It brings the quarrel to a screaming halt, and then the real issue (which could be scary, could end the relationship, could show some weakness in him) doesn't have to be dealt with.

Violence also works as an outlet for frustration. Being a teenager is about the most frustrating thing going, what with parents, teachers, coaches, principals, guidance counselors, peers, and everybody else and his mother putting the pressure on. The frustration builds, the guy lashes out, and suddenly he's energized. It feels good to go with both fists, almost like a drug. And as with a drug, it's tempting to give himself over again and again to something that makes him feel that good. That's why some guys feel the need for a release first and *then* look for something they think justifies a violent reaction—like a girlfriend who wore too much eyeshadow today or something equally trivial.

Violence also works in that, ten to one, the person who uses it gets his own way as a result. Some people (girls included!) grow up basing their lives on the assumption that the only purpose of other people is to cater to them. If someone doesn't cater, especially a partner in love, they're likely to throw a tantrum, especially if that has worked since they were two years old. Unfortunately, a sixteen-year-old boy probably isn't going to throw himself on the floor and cry. It's more probable that he'll slam things around, peel out in his car—or rap his neglecting girlfriend in the mouth.

And once he has his way, he also has power, something the violent person seems to crave. He has shown his victim that it can happen again. He has shown her who's in charge. He's so insecure that he probably suspects that if he doesn't come on strong he'll be victimized, too, so he irritates his girlfriend deliberately and then pounces on her when she reacts, setting up an opportunity to defend his self-image.[1] This is no uncontrollable impulse. It's conscious, and what's more, it's useful.

Reason #2: It arises from mistaken beliefs about being male.
The idealized "real man":

* never fails;
* never walks away from a fight;
* is tough, strong, aggressive, daring, and brave;
* doesn't express his feelings;
* is never vulnerable; never cries (is never a "sissy" or a "wimp");
* is capable and knows how to cope;
* is in charge;
* is independent;
* in no way ever acts, thinks, or feels anything like a woman.

One psychologist says a great many American boys are raised on the basis of four phrases:[2]

1. "No sissy stuff"—no crying, no hysteria, no admitting you're in pain.
2. "Be a big wheel"—be #1, the one everyone else looks up to, king of the mountain (remembering, of course, that as king of the mountain you have to continually fight for your rightful place at the top).
3. "Be a sturdy oak"—don't show any weakness, and for heaven's sake don't ask for help!
4. "Give 'em hell"—show your true strength by being physical.

Let's face it, that's a completely unrealistic set of expectations to have to live up to. A guy sometimes feels weak, passive, and out of control just like everyone else, and having no room to make mistakes and be human puts him in an awful bind. He has none of the occasional retreats back into childhood that girls have. How many teenage guys do you know who still cuddle up to their moms and dads as girls do, who can leap onto their parents' bed after an evening out to fill them in on his romantic triumphs the way a girl does? A girl can camouflage her journey into womanhood with brief jumps back into little-girlhood. A boy can't.

So he can keep grabbing for power in everything, including his relationships, to fulfill the manly ideal and appear strong. Sooner or later, however, all those emotions he's hiding are going to burst out in the only feeling he's allowed to have according to the male code, and that's anger.

But, of course, that's all right, society says, because anger and its expression, violence, prove masculinity, daring, courage, and aggressiveness. Wild, isn't it? He's using violence as an outlet for his sense of rage at an unfair world in which he can never live up to the expectations of being masculine, and while he's doing it, he's *proving* that he *is* a man![3]

Society has never helped the situation much. Since the earliest recorded times, men have been told they *have* to take charge of the women in their lives if they are to be real men. Consider these *Rules of Marriage*, compiled by Friar Cherubino Siena between 1450 and 1481: "Scold [your wife] sharply, bully and terrify her. And if this still doesn't work—take up a stick and beat her soundly."[4] So is it any wonder that if a girl attacks a boy's masculinity he feels justified in proving he's masculine by using an "acceptable" masculine response—violence? And the same if *she* fails to live up to accepted standards of what a girlfriend should be (dependent, obedient, and dumb, perhaps?)? One study done with battering men in Massachusetts showed that most didn't hold themselves at all responsible for their behavior. They blamed their women victims for not measuring up to their expectations.[5]

Girls being the more independent, more outspoken people they've become in recent years, those expectations are being met less and less. If a guy still buys into the traditional rules for what's feminine and what's masculine, he's going to struggle with the constant burden of having to be buff, rough, and tough *and* with being denied what he feels are his legitimate rights. Men are as much the victims of the macho mentality as women[6], and the more they adhere to traditional sex-role expectations, the more likely they are to approve of and use violence against the females in their personal relationships.

Reason #3: It satisfies the need for control.

If you don't think each of us is born with the need to control our environment, take a look at a two-day-old baby screaming in his crib, and watch everybody tear around grabbing diapers and bottles and pacifiers!

Showing possession and displaying power become even more real and natural for a teenager. Some do it with noisy cars. Some do it by showing affection in public. That's okay, because learning control over *your* life is a healthy thing. But learning control over *another person's* life is not.

When a guy tries to take control of his girlfriend, he may do it so he'll feel in control of himself. Or he may do it because he can't control the people who are really controlling him—the coach, the teacher, his parents. In the case of sexual abuse and rape, he may do it out of a need to overpower and humiliate someone else because *he* feels overpowered and humiliated. Violence happens when a person can't satisfy his need for power in normal ways—success in school, leadership positions, chances to make decisions. If he doesn't have enough self-esteem to run his own life, or if the ability to be himself is being blocked by somebody or something (parents want him to be a football player instead of a musician, for example), anger, rage, and hate will arise, and he's probably going to vent those on somebody susceptible—somebody like his girlfriend.

This factor of control becomes more powerful once violence starts to occur in the relationship. To continue to make him feel in charge, the violence has to increase each time. And because he's treating his girlfriend cruelly, the boy knows she's bound to try to leave him sooner or later, and that fear causes him to try to get *greater* control over her. The need to have that power seems bottomless. He may even say, "If only she'd change this, this, and this, I wouldn't have to be mean to her." But the list is endless.

Reason #4: It's the result of emotional dependence on the girl.

It may sound strange to say that a guy who's abusive to his girlfriend is dependent on her, but it's often true.

One of the basic characteristics of the "real man," if you recall, is that he isn't supposed to have feelings other than anger. But of course he *does*. He's a human being! He can't own up to those feelings, though, because to show hurt, sadness, or disappointment would be tantamount to social suicide. You just don't see guys sitting around in the locker room or standing around the pool table discussing their emotions the way girls do around a set of electric curlers. You start opening up to your male friends about your weaknesses and insecurities and somebody might not understand. Somebody might think you're a wimp. Somebody might think you're gay!

But if a guy has a girlfriend, he can displace his feelings onto her. He starts to expect her to know how he feels and what will make him feel better. He expects her to take care of him and thinks he has a right to blame her when he feels lousy. Pretty soon he starts to see her as part of himself, so naturally he thinks he can't live without her. If she asserts a little independence or turns her attention to other people or things, even for a minute, he feels he's losing part of himself, and he's scared. To hold onto her, he terrorizes her. To keep her away from other people who might take her (and him!) away, he tries to isolate her. As a result, she becomes less and less able to cope with anything or anyone else, and *she* becomes dependent on *him*. That's reassuring to him, so he does it some more. Pretty soon they have love and caring all intertwined with pain, jealousy, and absolute control. Where there should be laughter and kisses and the holding of hands, there's humiliation, intimidation, and beatings, all done in the name of love.

When they're so overinvolved in each other's lives and their only security comes from each other, the couple's breakup could threaten the very core of their existence. The holding on becomes more and more desperate and more and more violent.

Those are the basic reasons why guys turn to violence in their relationships. They're complicated, though, and hard to change, so society tends to look for easier, more concrete things to blame. But those other things aren't reasons, they're just contributing factors. Since they do add to the problem, let's take a look at them.

Pressure and Frustration

If you've lived a day as a teenager, you've felt pressured and frustrated. There are parental expectations. Peer pressure. Too much freedom you may not be ready to handle. Sexual activity. The presence of drugs. Divorce in the family. Emphasis on academic achievement. The knowledge explosion—more to know and a greater demand for technical knowledge. Disillusionment and uncertainty about things you always believed in. Financial problems. Physical changes and growth, new and confusing sexual urges, and emotions that can seem to rock the world. To make matters worse, many parents and even physicians aren't sensitive to the stresses that teenagers feel.[7] And of course, in adolescence you're in a kind of purgatory between childhood and adulthood. Some days you don't know *who* you are, and that can make your sense of self pretty shaky.[8] Throw in a steady dating relationship, and you've got an earthquake on your hands. Maybe you feel inferior to the person you're dating for some reason (family, social status, etc.). Maybe your girlfriend can outtalk you any day of the week. Maybe she's hostile and aggressive. Maybe she nags, calls names, uses profanity, throws insults, makes verbal attacks on your weaknesses. She doesn't cause the violence, but she can sure add fuel to the already smoldering fire.

When the pressure mounts within a teenager, his natural immaturity (which is okay because, darn it, he isn't an adult yet and shouldn't expect himself to be!) makes it tough for him to delay his response and take time to cool off. He may blow immediately. Or he may let it build up over time and then discharge it all in one big explosion. In either case, he turns his internal confusion and stress out on the world, and because he has learned that violence is a legitimate way for a man to deal with anger, frustration, and stress, he goes for it. In fact, he may not know any way to express his feelings except through violence. He literally feels that he has no choice.

The Media

Seeing violence on television doesn't make you go out and smack somebody up the side of the head, but it sure makes it easier for you to accept that action in yourself or in someone else. You've seen it so much on the tube, the movie screen, and the video cassette, you may have become desensitized.

And no wonder! America seems to have a permanent taste for violence,[9] so much so that violence on television alone has increased 65 percent since 1980 and is found in 46 percent of all music videos (almost half of these containing violence between men and women).[10] We actually *saw* the rape in "Once Upon a Time in America." We saw the heart torn out of a still-living man in "Indiana Jones and the Temple or Doom." In the Twisted Siser video of "We're Not Gonna Take It" we saw a boy point his electric guitar at his father, releasing a force that blasted his dad through the wall. In the video "Faces of Death" we saw a veritable anthology of dismemberment, execution, cannibalism, and animal slaughter.[11] There is an entire genre of visual entertainment known as "slice-and-dice" films—like "Friday the Thirteenth" and "Halloween"— whose primary target audience is males of high school and college age. Those are our dating men, friends.

By age eighteen the average young adult has seen 50,000 murders or attempted murders on TV alone, and statistics are not available yet on how much violent pornography he or she has seen on the pages of *Hustler* and *Penthouse*, in the flickers of rock videos depicting women in chains and cages, in the R-rated slice-and-dice movies now available on video cassettes and cable TV that invariably show a sexual scene immediately preceding each murder—and provide an unmistakable link between sex and violence. Violent pornography (defined by eighteen-year-old college freshman Wendy Bowers as that which depicts actions against another human in which physical violence or physical injury is part of the sexual act, enjoyment, or gratification[12]) blends violence with sex. When that happens in a young mind, sexual pleasure becomes connected with abuse, pain, and violence, and the damage is devastating. There's less empathy for victims of abuse. The idea that women enjoy violence becomes prevalent. People start accepting violence as the first alternative in a conflict.

Even sexually explicit movies without violence can cause unrealistic expectations that will frustrate a guy into choosing violence as a release. Here's a quote that says it all:

> On the screen, heaving voluptuaries make every moment seem rife with unsurpassable pleasure. Encounters continue for longer than most professional football games, but never is there a time out, never a dropped pass or blocked field goal, never a line plunge that falls short. By the time adolescent video fans reach the age of majority, the recollection of so many X-rated conquests may make their own efforts seem strictly small time.[13]

All that sexual innuendo as standard fare is tough on the girls, too. Magazines, books, and popular songs urge them to be sexy and never back them up if they want to say no. Date rape thus becomes standard procedure. The boy takes no as a personal rejection, his resentment builds because his expectations aren't being fulfilled, and he finally figures he has waited long enough.

Again, the media doesn't *cause* dating violence. A person with a stable home life and good models for relationships in parents might not be accepting of violence no matter what he or she sees on TV. But if other conditions are right, an ultra-gore film can act as a trigger.

Drugs and Alcohol

Drugs and alcohol are often the scapegoats for the violence choice, but as we've said before their use is usually an excuse or cover-up for actions that are bound to take place as soon as some blame can be invented. Yes, alcohol allows a guy to let down his inhibitions and become violent. Drugs in the downer category do cause hostility, and those in the upper group cause aggression. But the user is still in control. He chooses to use the stuff, knowing it nudges him toward violence. And he doesn't beat everyone else up while drunk or drugged. He saves it as a little something special just for her! Sorry—but he can control both his substance abuse and his violence. It isn't easy, but help is available.

Sports

Wait a minute! Sports are supposed to be a healthy outlet, aren't they? Yes, and they can be. But a boy who is already prone to be physical learns the language of violence in sports. "Get out there and tear them up." "Kill the quarterback!" "Kick some butt." He learns to release tension and anxiety and to express friendship in rough play, so it's more likely that he'll express his anger, frustration, and fear through violence. He also learns through competition that somebody always has to *win*—and it had better be him.

That doesn't mean sports are bad. For Pete's sake, every Heisman trophy winner is not out there beating up his wife! But what an impressionable guy can learn from his participation in sports can be bad stuff if it isn't balanced in the rest of his life.

Violence in the Family

Although they are not the only ones engaging in relationship violence, batterers are frequently people who come from violent homes, or at least homes having a general lack of respect for women and children and very few constructive ways to express emotions. Sons of wife-beaters often grow up to beat their own female companions, and daughters grow up with an expectation that they will be beaten. As many as 50 percent of girls who are raised in violent families will be victims of battering, while 60 percent of the boys will become batterers at some time.[14]

It isn't hard to see why that happens. Abuse by boys who were themselves abused gives them back the power that was taken from them. Boys who have seen abuse used on their mothers learn from modeling that violence is the only path for settling arguments or maintaining a superior position. Because *his* girlfriend is probably more assertive and independent than his mother, he will have to fight harder for power. But he'll do it, because he has learned growing up that he has a right to.

Even in families where the discipline used is not by the standards of the court "abusive," violence can be learned. Studies have shown that physical punishment by parents increases rather than decreases aggression in children and makes them more likely to turn around and hit someone else when they become frustrated or angry.[15] Violence causes more violence, no matter what the motive in the first place, and with 84 percent to 97 percent of American families using physical punishment at some point, the potential is pretty scary. That's a lot of girls learning that those who love them the most are also those who have a right to hit them. That's a lot of boys learning that when something is really important it justifies the use of physical force.

It isn't just the physical stuff in families that's doing it; it's verbal violence as well, from parents *and* offspring. "The freedom to express anger in words has become one of the sacred rights of American kids,"[16] writes a psychologist. There's arguing and sticking up for one's rights, which is called confronting and asserting. Then there's cussing, swearing, and hurling humiliating epithets, which is called verbal violence. If it isn't considered wrong in the family to insult or yell and scream at another person, it won't be considered wrong in any other relationship, and the verbal violence may ultimately build to physical abuse.

If your parents use any of the above on you or each other, I wouldn't suggest running to them and advising them that they've turned you into a potential batterer. I would just be aware that the things you've learned in your upbringing, even though your parents probably did the very best they knew how, could put you in a high-risk group.

Other Family Problems

Even model teens from "nice" families can turn on each other. Maybe they've been suppressing anger for years at being overprotected and not allowed to make decisions. Maybe they've had too many demands made on them.

Maybe they've been criticized too much and recognized and loved too little. Maybe their parents love them but have been emotionally unavailable because of their own problems or because they have to work long hours. Maybe they've had too much freedom and had to grow up too early. Those things can build up and explode.

The high rate of divorce doesn't help. Forty percent of all young people in the United States will experience the effects of divorce by age eighteen.[17] That makes them more vulnerable to stress. Statistically, children of divorce are more likely to become involved with alcohol and drugs, commit suicide, get in trouble with the law, and fail in school. A Boston study even showed a higher incidence of sexual abuse among kids with parents who have divorced and remarried.[18]

Even if none of those more obvious problems comes to pass, a teen with divorced parents often suffers from too early having to play a counseling role to a parent or at least may have to deal with his own problems while his parents temporarily become kids themselves. Pile the parents' helplessness on top of the kid's painful feelings, and a lack of real trust in relationships is bound to be the result.

It can't be said too many times: What causes a boy to use violence is that he chooses to use violence. He doesn't have to be under the influence of stress, alcohol, or his father. He just has to decide it's the way to go. Whether he's you, your boyfriend, someone you know, or someone you're afraid you'll become, please read on and see how you can help him stop.

CHAPTER ◇ 5

Why Girls Stay

Sara had her nose broken twice—by the same boy—
before she was twenty. Jamie was slapped around
and called names like "whore" and "slut" by boyfriend Greg her entire senior year. Kathleen at twenty-one
married the fiancé who had been verbally and sexually
assaulting her since they were eighteen.

The common response to stories like these is, "Why do
they stay? If they don't get out, isn't it as much their fault
as it is the guys'?"

The answer to the second question is a flat-out, freeze-
dried, fat-fried "NO!" It isn't their fault. A guy has chosen
to abuse. That's his responsibility. His girlfriend's choice
to stay with him doesn't lessen that responsibility. *Her*
responsibility is only for herself.

Then why doesn't she take it? Why does she stay? There
are a number of reasons, and in this chapter we'll go into
them. It is hoped that it will create some understanding for
the girl who feels trapped in an abusive relationship and is
hearing, "I don't have any sympathy for her. Why doesn't
she just get out?"—the very kinds of comments that keep
her hiding her pain. Try very hard to remember as you
read that:

1. *over*analyzing the girl can put the focus in the wrong place; it's the boy, the batterer, who needs the most long-term help;
2. reasons that may seem stupid or ridiculous to someone who isn't locked into a knock-down-drag-out relationship are very real to someone who is.

Reason #1: She's humiliated and ashamed.

Probably nothing is more degrading than being deliberately hurt by someone who supposedly loves you— unless it's having to admit that it's happening. Kathi recalls looking around at her friends and seeing them in their "perfect" boy-girl things and thinking, "There must be something wrong with me. I can't let anybody see that our relationship is this bad." The shame and embarrassment cause many girls to go into hiding with their battering. Only an estimated one in ten females reports assault by boyfriend or husband to the police or a women's shelter.[1] That same sense of humiliation can even cause them to deny to themselves that it's happening. Overwhelmed with humiliation, shock, and fear, they find it's more comfortable to pretend it never took place or that it isn't so bad. They even find themselves rationalizing that when the relationship is good it's *good*, and that outweighs the bad.

This crime—and it *is* a crime—is the type, like rape by a stranger or incest, that shames the victim. To stay and tough it out may seem preferable to saying, "This happened to me, and I had to leave."

Reason #2: She thinks she can change him.

Some girls have the fantasy that they can transform Mr. Wrong into Mr. Right. Elizabeth Fishel, author of *The Men in Our Lives*, writes about the girl with this dream:

Her secret hope is that the sheer force of her will or charm or simply perseverance will soothe the angry brow of her lover, undo his inaccessibility, secure his heart forever.[2]

An abuser, in spite of his macho front, can often be very childlike and needy, and that appeals to the strong, compassionate girl who wants someone to take care of. Usually after an incident of battering there's a period of remorse when a guy may even cry as he begs his girlfriend not to leave him and promises to try to change if only she'll help him. That can be pretty hard to turn your back on, even when your nose is bleeding or you're holding several of your teeth in your hand.

Laurel, a fifteen-year-old sophomore, found it very hard, and her story may help explain this syndrome. Her boyfriend, Chris, was *Teen* magazine cover material. Even at sixteen, he was six foot two and tipped the scales at 206, every inch of it pure brawn. His haunting good looks—deep-set brown eyes, dark hair that fell over his forehead in a rebellious tumble faintly reminiscent of James Dean—were enhanced by his tough-guy image. He played football, was into skiing, and could hold his own with a hunting rifle.

And he was magnetic. The Red Sea of the high school hall parted when he passed through, and girls, so Laurel said, "dropped at his feet." He was used to getting what he wanted, and he never did anything halfway, including woo Laurel. It was a heady feeling, and from her position on the pedestal (where an oxygen mask was very nearly necessary) she looked down on the world through starry eyes.

But the stars didn't blind her to the Chris that was slowly emerging. She discovered that he was quite the partier, into booze and marijuana and an occasional snort of cocaine. But when she balked at that, Chris was persuasive. He told her he wanted to get off drugs and stop drinking, and he wanted her to help him. He pleaded with her to stay with him, because she was the only one who could set him right again.

That appealed to Laurel's compassionate side. Armed with his promise to stay off the stuff, she made sure he went to every class, tucked his books under his arm for him everyday after school, and talked him through his homework over the phone. She found herself worrying as much about his grades as she did her own, but it seemed to be paying off. Chris was passing every class, and his friends marveled at the "changes" in him.

Yet other hidden sides of Chris didn't change, no matter what Laurel did. He was possessive and over protective, jealous of anyone who talked to Laurel, including her girlfriends and her family. He went into black moods and yelled uncontrollably. When Laurel argued back she found him grabbing her arm and screwing his fingers, hard, into her chin to make her look at him. There were the "purple passion" moods, too, when his demands for sex became frightening. When she got scared enough to say, "This is all smothering me, Chris," he threatened suicide. Not a day went by that he didn't tell her she was everything to him, that he needed her to help him change. Yet when she continued her campaign to keep him on the straight and narrow, he snarled that she was nagging him, and the cycle began again.

Finally she tried to break up with him. He threw her against a car and hit her in the stomach.

Yet although that *was* the end of their relationship, Laurel never told anyone. She still cared. She still wanted to help. She still didn't want to get him into trouble.

Reason #3: She thinks the battering is her fault.

Often batterers are guys like Chris who have a carefully cultivated charm that everybody loves. If the guy is so popular and respected and yet so different with his girlfriend, what is she to believe but that she is somehow bringing out the Mr. Hyde side of his otherwise pleasant Dr. Jekyll personality? That, of course, is reinforced by nice, friendly, normally sympathetic people who unintentionally conspire to make the victim feel at fault. "Any man can be driven to rage by a bitchy woman." "He's such a nice guy, you'd have to go a long way to make him mad." "I'm so jealous of you for having Kevin (Keith, or Kenny). He's such a doll—I bet you guys never fight." And then there's the guy himself who, as one girl puts it, "is so good at saying 'It's your fault.' So good I believed it."

Put all that on a girl who has been brought up with a strong sense of responsibility and who believes the myths—

- Failure in a relationship means failure as a woman.
- Girls must be nurturers and expend their energy in supporting boys to achieve success.
- It's the woman's responsibility to keep things cool and on an even keel.
- If I could be better, he'd stop.

—and you've got a girl who feels more guilt than the guy does! She is willing to do just about anything to make things better, and she believes that no one can help her do it but herself. A relationship to her means going through everything together, and she'll put up with the bruises and the insults and the fear, all the while trying to figure out how she's "making him lose control." Never once does she consider that he's the one with the problem, not she.

Reason #4: She's immobilized by her low self-esteem.

Everybody feels rocky about their self-image when they're teenagers. It's in the adolescent contract to have a kind of slippery, shapeless sense of identity. Much of being thirteen-to-nineteen is figuring out who you are and how you can make yourself feel good about you, and a teenager looks for that in a number of places. One of the most important is in the arms of a member of the opposite sex. Adolescent love *is* a search for the self.[3]

However, that part of the quest can get a girl into trouble if:

- she doubts her own worth so much that she feels she deserves and needs to be punished somehow;
- she thinks she's not complete or successful or secure without a guy, no matter how good she is at other things;
- she's very susceptible to criticism;
- she's afraid to be herself and tries to be what other people want her to be;
- she constantly lets other people give her directions because she isn't sure where she wants to go or whether she can get there;
- she's certain she can't stand alone.

If a girl who's having a hard time with those kinds of thoughts teams up with a guy who abuses, she's going to have one heck of a time prying herself out of the relationship. The abuse itself, particularly the verbal type in which she's repeatedly told she's awful and incapable, will chisel away at her sense of identity even more until it has simply eroded into fear and helplessness.

If you're a guy or you're a strong girl with a firm sense of self, you may be having a tough time understanding all this. But you've probably been afraid of something at some time in your life, and if you have, you know that fear immobilizes. It keeps you from thinking clearly and acting in a reasonable way. Let's face it, you do weird things when you're afraid. A person who hasn't yet learned to think of herself as important and worthy and special is afraid all the time. She's scared and she freezes and she can't go anywhere. She reacts just as you did when your house was on fire or your favorite uncle was dying or the brakes went out on your car. Sure, she needs to work on how she feels about herself. But just because she feels lousy about herself right now, so that she can't free herself from the guy who's beating her, doesn't mean it's okay for him to do it!

Reason #5: She's scared spitless.

When Laurel told Chris she wanted to break up, he threw her against a parked vehicle and drove a first into her abdomen. When Nancy told Lance she wanted to break up, he punched open a wall and then chased her all the way to her car. When Suzanne told Tony she wanted to break up, he told her she'd never get away from him, that he'd hunt her down and haunt her for the rest of her life.

Enough said?

How a girl gets to a place where those reasons can be enough to keep her in a torturous thing that's supposed to be love is something else entirely. If we could figure that out, we'd probably have the problem licked. A few possibilities, though, are worth looking at.

The Presence—or Absence—of Violence in Her Own Family

In a study done at California State University, Sacramento, with a large group of high school students, 51 percent said they came from homes where violence was used in some form.[4] Another study done at the University of New Hampshire with 385 students revealed that 16 percent had actually witnessed physical violence between their mothers and fathers during the previous year.[5] An estimated two million children are abused annually in the United States.[6]

Having to cope with violence too early in life can cause a girl to accept it when it comes along later in her personal experience. Men are supposed to hit women, she thinks. Being hit is at least attention. This is the way relationships are. Why should mine be any different? As a result, an estimated 66 percent of women who see violence at home as girls become victims themselves later in life.[7]

For those who have never experienced violence, its occurrence with a boyfriend will come as a shock. If she isn't aware that it does happen, she's totally unprepared and probably doesn't know what to do. This didn't happen to my mother, she thinks. What am I doing wrong?

It's important to remember that childhood abuse or seeing parents' violence are not important overall *causes* of a girl's abuse by a lover. That's another form of blaming the victim that we need to get rid of. Its presence in her experience just helps us understand why a girl might stay and suffer with an abusive relationship.

The Way She Was Brought Up

In their analysis of 160,000 teenagers, Jane Norman and psychologist Myron Harris concluded that a father's treatment of his daughter has a great deal to do with her attitudes toward men.[8]

- If Daddy treated her like a fragile doll and expected her to be pretty and ladylike, she grew up thinking she was incompetent to take care of herself and had to rely on a man for her identity.
- If her father made all her decisions and kept the controls tight at all times, she'll have a hard time listening to her own voice when it tells her she's being mistreated by a guy.
- If her dad was timid and hesitant and passive, she has come to think of the world as a scary, unmanageable place. She's easy prey for the abusive boy.
- If Pops was a charmer and groomed her for social triumph without nourishing her creative side, she is probably convinced that finding a guy is life's major quest and will do what it takes to keep one.
- If Papa was erratic and inconsistent in his treatment of her, her trust in other people is undermined, and she may have trouble finding other dependable relationships. She may accept irrational behavior.

That is not to say that every girl reading this book should run to her father and tell him he has messed her up big time! Nobody teaches a dad how to be a dad. The fathers get even less parenthood training than the mothers do, which is practically nil. He did his best. It's your turn to deal with who you are now, and with a little understanding of where you came from, you can. Whoever you are and however you were brought up, you don't deserve to be abused. No one does.

What Society Says

What society says is that violence is okay. It's accepted. It's expected. Sylvester Stallone does it. Dad does it. And when the boy next door does it, that must be all right, too. Somehow, even in a society where women are becoming stronger, more independent, more aware of their rights, it still seems that taking a stand against male brutality violates some notion of "womanhood." When the TV shows, the movies, the radio and magazine ads, the videos are all saying, "Men are tough—women are soft—a woman has to have a tough man to be a soft woman," it's hard to see a bruised arm or a bruised sense of self-esteem as a reason for leaving.

It *is* hard to leave. We'll talk about how it can be done in a later chapter. Right now, let's turn to another step, something that's a little less painful. Let's talk about how to *avoid* getting into the mire of an abusive relationship in the first place.

CHAPTER ◇ 6

Avoiding Abuse

L aurel saw the handwriting on the wall in her relationship with Chris and got out before she was seriously
hurt. If she had known how to avoid getting tangled
up in that kind of bad-news situation at the outset, she
could have saved herself the emotional scars she did end
up with. But how do you do that?

If you're a teenage girl, you have one chance in two of
picking a guy to marry who won't physically abuse you.
You have only one chance in ten of picking one who won't
emotionally abuse you.[1] Those aren't great odds, nor are
they easy to beat even if you know what to look for. You
realize that the danger signs include jealousy, a macho
image, punching friends—but good grief, that's adolescent
behavior! Just about every teenage boy does that stuff at
some point. How do you separate the batterers from the
guys who are just—being guys?

Again, it's no simple matter. But a few guidelines *can*
help. Even if you never meet up with a potential abuser,
following them can insure that any relationship you have
will be a healthy one.

Guideline #1: Learn to love yourself before you fall in love with someone else.

There's a wonderful saying that arose from the women's movement: "A woman without a man is like a fish without a bicycle."

It's fun to go out with guys, have flowers sent to you, have a special person to share the ups and downs with. A good relationship is a wonderful thing, but it's important not to think that unless you have one you're nothing. Know who you are, like who you are, know what you want, and be able to go for it.

That means having control over your own life.

That means enjoying being alone sometimes.

That means staying clear of self-disgust.

That means knowing what you believe in.

That means feeling secure even when there's no one beside you.

It means knowing your possibilities and not letting anyone stand in the way of your achieving them.

If you can do all that, you're a whole person. When you're whole, you won't let anyone abuse you.

Guideline #2: Know your rights in a relationship and stand up for them.

You have a right:

- to share equally in descisions;
- to grow and explore your own potential;
- to have other friends;
- to express your opinions and to have them given respect and consideration;
- to have your feelings about sex respected;
- to have your emotional, physical, and intellectual

needs be as important as those of your partner;
- to expect your partner to give 50 percent in resolving differences;
- to hold him responsible for his behavior rather than assuming that responsibility yourself;
- to act in a way that's best for you;
- to make or refuse a request;
- to change your mind;
- not to be physically, emotionally, or sexually abused;
- not to blame yourself entirely if the relationship in which you've invested love and effort ends.

Know those rights. Believe them. Say them out loud to your boyfriend if you have to. Remember that failure to allow you those rights is abuse. Don't accept a violation under any circumstances. If he can't handle it, it's time to get out. Right away—before a rough shove, a twisted arm, a rude comment, or a threat to your self-esteem escalates into more severe punishment.

Your boyfriend has the same rights you do, and of course it's only fair and healthy to the relationship to respect them. However, at the risk of sounding like a broken record, if you violate his rights he has the right to call you on it, and he has the right to leave; he doesn't have the right to abuse you because of it.

Guideline #3: Be aware of the danger signs.

Unless you know something about relationship abuse, it's sometimes hard to recognize an abuser. Who would go out with somebody who openly admitted that he beat up girls or who approached the first date with, "You're going out with me or I'll rip off your lips!"? It doesn't happen that way!

Besides, there is no one abusive "type" to be on the

lookout for. Guys who hit aren't always bullies or macho men. Though some are loudly aggressive, others are basically passive in public. Many are attractive and popular. Some are even model students from model families.

But there are indications that a guy could become cruel to a girlfriend. If you see these in a boy whom you're dating or who is interested in you, it's a good idea to back off and at least take another look:

- He has an explosive temper, even though it's not directed at you.
- Minor situations like being jostled in a crowd or having to stand in line cause him to blow.
- When he's angry he breaks or throws things.
- He seems to believe that woman was born to serve man. Maybe he's disrespectful to his mother or gives you a lot of orders.
- He makes comments that indicate that women are innately stupid. ("Oh, God, it's a woman driver, no wonder.")
- He puts other people down a great deal.
- He's mean to animals or children.
- He pressures you for dates.
- He's excessively charming (overkill with cards, notes, flowers, candy, gifts).
- He talks about "taking care of you."
- He consistently dates girls a lot younger than he is.
- He has a reputation for fighting with other guys over past girlfriends.
- He expresses all emotions as anger (puts his fist through a wall when he's sad, peels out in his car when he's disappointed, pounds a table when he's scared, lashes out when his feelings are hurt).
- He doesn't control his impulses (takes the dare to

drag race, can be easily influenced to get drunk, wants sex and wants it *now*).

- He uses pornography (*Hustler* magazine in his bathroom, X-rated movies with the guys).
- He always blames his failures and disappointments on other people.
- He's often resentful, suspicious, moody, and tense.
- He's very competitive and can't stand to lose at anything.
- He has trouble putting his feelings into words.
- He's a definite Dr. Jekyll-Mr. Hyde.
- He appears to be the life of the party but on closer inspection is really a loner. Doesn't have deep, committed friendships.
- He likes to impress people—especially you.
- He shows low self-esteem (perhaps by being sloppy, jealous, controlling).

Just because a boy has one or two of those traits doesn't mean he's a batterer. No one is perfect, surely, and if you wouldn't go out with a guy unless he was, you might as well become a nun! But if the list pretty much fits, I'd be wary. He has the potential to blow—at you—when the going gets tough.

If you're already going with a guy, it's a good idea to take a close look at your developing relationship. If these danger signals flash at you, be careful:

- He becomes resentful when you assert yourself.
- He gets very frustrated when there's any trouble between you.
- When you argue, he makes threats, calls names, and won't consider your point of view.

- He sometimes raises his hand to you as if he's going to hit you.
- He insists on sex or even intimacy when you don't want it.
- He wants you to change basic things about yourself.
- You're uncomfortable about communicating with him on sensitive subjects.
- You aren't really yourself when you're with him because you're afraid to be.
- He gets violent when you're playing (tickles too hard, wrestles too roughly, gets ticked off if you beat him at tennis).
- He refuses to share responsibility in your relationship (for solving problems, for example).
- He likes to take charge—of you, of the social situations you're in.
- You feel as if he owns you, or would like to. He's extremely jealous and possessive.
- He tells you your friends are no good for you, that they're the wrong crowd.
- He says he hates himself and is whole only when he's with you.

There may be some things you really like about this guy and your relationship with him. You need to ask yourself: Is that worth the injury he could do to my self-esteem? That kind of damage is long term. As poet Alice Walker puts it, "Never offer your heart to someone who eats hearts."[2]

Guideline #4: Take it slow in any relationship.
Many times abuse occurs in a relationship in which the couple have made a commitment and are sexually intimate.

This kind of relationship is the toughest to break off, no matter what mistreatment is going on. So part of avoiding a violent relationship is getting to know the guy well—*very* well—before you get in too deep.

—That can be tough. We're trained from an early age to look for one special person with whom to share our lives, and the teen years unfortunately become a time for directing the lion's share of emotional energy toward finding that partner. It's easy to become preoccupied with finding a *mate* and to start looking at guys as people who could possibly fill that role, rather than as unique human beings. The whole thing becomes an act or a game and takes on a phoniness that doesn't belong in love. If either partner starts the "game" by feigning interest in the other person's likes or playing masculine or feminine roles they really don't fit into, trouble can start when their real identities emerge. That's when it can become apparent that the guy who seemed so nice at the beginning is demanding, jealous, and contemptuous of women.

There is one basic rule in love: Be yourself always. Do nothing to win someone over that is contrary to who you are. If you act like yourself right from the start and give your dating partner a chance to relax and show his true colors before you commit to a steady relationship or get involved sexually, your chances are much greater of avoiding abuse *and* of having a healthier, more meaningful thing going.

It's a good idea to zero in a little on the issue of your sexual relationship. Movies and TV these days seem to be saying that casual sex can't hurt you if you're both mature, consenting individuals. In a word, that's pigwash.

Unless the two people involved know each other intimately and are committed to their relationship, sex *can* hurt. It can turn a first date into an exclusive, permanent arrangement neither person is ready for (but both submit to out of guilt—"It's okay! It's special"). It can lead to frustration because it isn't providing the warmth and security its participants were seeking. It can fool people into thinking they know each other or that they love each other when they don't. It can provide the leverage a guy (or a girl) needs to hang on when the hanging on is no good.

So how do you know when you've got this mature relationship where the two people really know each other? How do you know you're not on a collision course? Here are some questions that might help you. Answer them honestly for yourself.

- Does each of you have a secure belief in your own value? yes
- Do you both have other meaningful personal friendships outside your relationship? yes
- Are you beyond being possessive or jealous of each other's growth and expansion? yes
- Are you friends as well as lovers? yes
- Does each of you feel like a whole person when you're alone? no
- Have you both maintained the interests you had before you met? yes
- Can you imagine still being friends if you were no longer totally involved with each other? yes
- Are you both better people as a result of the relationship? yes

Developing a relationship so that you can answer yes to all of those questions requires time and shared experiences and feelings. It means getting to know each other as real people rather than ideals, and it means dealing with the conflict and stress and changes that occur when you find out that nobody lives happily ever after. It's a matter of finally seeing each other with no pretenses and all defenses down, liking what you see, and feeling good about yourself because you do. It's worth the wait, because abuse isn't likely to happen in a relationship like that.

If the relationship you're in is totally selfish on either side, if either of you is concerned primarily with your own needs and neither of you is looking to see if you really *like* the other person, the potential for abuse is high. In this kind of relationship, your energy is depleted instead of fed. Constant fighting, petty jealousies, and lots of insecurities abound. You tend to smother each other, never allowing the other person to grow as an individual for fear that he or she will outgrow the relationship. That's not intimacy. That's addiction. That's abuse.

You have to make your own decisions about the sexual side of this, but here's a word of advice if you want to avoid devastating personal violence. Don't behave in an intimate way without an intimate relationship. It can be hard when you're young and the juices are flowing, but if you want to say no you have a right to, and you *can*. Try these approaches:

- "You're terrific. I like you a lot. But when I have sex, it's got to mean a total commitment, and we aren't there yet."
- "I respect your feelings, so I ask you to respect my choice. Let's not."
- "You say you love me. If you do, you won't pressure me. I'm not ready."

Be aware, too, that violence occurs even more frequently among single couples who live together. In a recent study at the University of New Hampshire it was found that cohabiting couples show higher levels of aggression than either dates or married people.[3] Having so much invested in the relationship and being isolated from family members makes it difficult to break up the relationship if abuse does occur. Although you may not be in a position to consider living with someone at this point, it's a good thing to keep in mind for the future.

Guideline #5: Follow the special guidelines for avoiding date rape.

Physical and emotional abuse often occur only in relationships that have been going on for a while. Sexual abuse has been known to happen even on the first date. It's called date rape, and it can hurt you sexually, physically, and mentally—for a long time. In her book *Safe, Strong, and Streetwise*, Helen Benedict says this about date rape: "If a boy wants sex from you and won't take no for an answer no matter how firm you are, that's assault. This is a boy who is so absorbed in himself that he doesn't care how you feel. All he wants is to feel powerful through sex and he's prepared to do anything to feel that, even to use violence."[4]

Here are some specific guidelines for limiting the chances of this kind of assault happening to you:

1. Know the danger signs of the sexually pushy guy— the one who likes to sit or stand too close and who enjoys your discomfort; the one who delivers the power stares; the one who blocks your way when you walk down the hall.
2. Know your sexual rights: You have a right to wait until you are ready for sex; you always have a right to say no; you have a right to be respected; you have a right to say yes to some sexual activities and

no to others; even if you've promised to make love and change your mind, you still have a right to say no.

3. Consider your rights carefully and decide right now what kind of intimacy you want with the people in your life. Don't wait until you're alone with a good-looking hunk who smells like British Sterling and is whispering wonderful things in your ear. Think about your limits while you're alone and calm.

4. Once you've decided on your sexual limits, stick to them. Make them clear to a date who's moving fast, and ask him to stop right away if he's headed for something you don't want. Don't wait, thinking he'll feel you tensing up and stop in a minute. Don't feel you've led him on and have some kind of obligation. Don't think—don't think anything! *React* to what you've thought through long before and stop him *now*. As Jim Long, editor of *Campus Life* magazine puts it, "Long-range happiness often follows the N-word: 'No.'"[5]

5. Make a deal with your parents. Ask them to pick you up whenever you call them for help wherever you are without getting mad at you. Even if it's late or you're somewhere you aren't supposed to be, it's better to face some consequences with them than to suffer being raped.

6. Exercise some control over the environment. Don't agree to be alone or go someplace secluded with a guy unless you really want to. Be particularly cautious if he's someone you don't know well or who's been pushy in the past.

7. For your own safety, be tactful when you say no. Don't imply that he's unattractive, uncouth,

nerdy, or unworthy of you. If in a panic you *do* tell him he's disgusting, that doesn't give him the right to force himself on you. Just try to avoid it as a precautionary measure. If tact obviously isn't going to work, then by all means get angry. It's okay to be rude to someone who's sexually pressuring you.

8. If someone is forcing you and none of the above works, try this. Let him think you want to but that you need to relax first or maybe go to the bathroom. Do anything that gives you a chance to get away, make a phone call, or have the safety of a crowd. When somebody won't take no, it's okay to pretend you want to in order to save yourself. Then *never* go out with him again.[6]

9. If you want to say no, say it in dress, talk, and action, too. Wear clothes that advertise yourself, not your sexiness. Cool down conversations that get too hot. Make suggestions to do fun things on dates, rather than ending up parking. You make it a whole lot easier on yourself if you don't invite the very thing you want to avoid.

This heap of advice may give you the idea that every guy is a potential batterer and rapist. On the contrary! There are enough healthy young relationships out there to attest to the fact that love—real love—is still one of the best things going. But abuse among dating couples is widespread enough to make it worth your while to be careful. Don't put the skids on dating and swear off men completely. Don't eye your date suspiciously every time he takes your arm to cross a street. Just know the guidelines and be aware. Then abuse can't sneak up on you and catch you in its trap.

Even if it has already, don't despair. Just read on.

CHAPTER 7

If You Are Being
Abused Now

I f you're currently being abused, you need to take some action right now.

That's a dangerous way to start this chapter, because one of the main characteristics of a violent relationship is denial. "He doesn't treat me all that good," the battered girl thinks, "but it isn't *that* bad. I mean, he's never broken any bones or anything."

So let's start by reviewing what it means to be battered. This chapter is for you if:

- you're frightened of your partner's temper at any time;
- you go along with whatever he wants for fear of arousing his anger;
- you apologize to other people for your partner's behavior when he treats you badly in front of them;
- you make decisions about activities and friends ac-

cording to what your partner wants or how your
partner will react;
- your partner has indicated that he thinks you're inferior, stupid, or undesirable—but keeps on seeing
  you and even telling you he loves you;
- you've been hit, kicked, shoved, or had things
  thrown at you by your partner;
- you've been pushed into sexual intimacy when you
  didn't want to and said you didn't want to.

If some or all of the above is making you feel shaky,
panicky, insecure, unstable, crazy, and alone most of the
time, that's cause for concern. Depression, tears, anger,
resentment—those are all signs that you're trapped in a
relationship that isn't good for you. You're being abused,
and it needs to stop.

Once you can accept that—which is no easy task in
itself—you need to remember two very important things.
If you have to take several days and just go over these two
things in your mind again and again before you take action,
do it. They're essential to your triumph over abuse.

1. *You have no reason to feel guilty for or ashamed of
what has happened to you.*

It has been said at least ten times in this book already,
but it bears repeating yet once more: If you are battered by
your boyfriend, it is in no way your fault.

It isn't your fault that you got hooked up with somebody
like him in the first place. No one's judgment is perfect
enough to foresee all danger.[1] Your trust has been violated,
and you're not to blame for that.

You didn't provoke him to hit you or hurl epithets at
you. He doesn't like or understand his *own* actions. The
provocation exists only in his mind, and probably what

triggered his attack on you really had nothing to do with you. You can't control that.

You don't deserve whatever you've been through, no matter what you think you might have done. If you teased him sexually, that wasn't kind, but it didn't warrant rape. No one—*no one*—should have to endure a forced and violent invasion of her personal and private self.[2] If you nagged him unmercifully, that wasn't cool, but it was no cause for physical violence. No one—*no one*—needs to be hit, slapped, or kicked to be taught a lesson. If you went out with other guys behind his back, that wasn't fair, but it doesn't mean you're a slut or a whore even if he called you one. No one—*no one*—has to be called names and thrown into a mental gutter. You may deserve anger, but you don't deserve violence.

Even if you've broken up a number of times and then gone back, you aren't "asking for it." No matter what you've done in the past, you have the right to make new choices now.

If you are ashamed and embarrassed because you've been battered and have decided it's all your fault, you've been trying to cope. You've done the best you could do. Now you can learn to handle it differently. *You are the victim.* Forgive yourself. Think of yourself kindly. Leslie Cantrell, author of a handbook for battered women, suggests that you say these things to yourself, over and over:

- I am not to blame for being abused.
- I am not causing my partner's abusive behavior.
- I don't like being abused.
- I don't have to take it.
- I am a lovable, valuable human being.
- I can decide what's best for me.
- I am a worthwhile person who can ask for help.

- As a human being and as a partner, I have the right to be treated with respect and love.[3]

2. *You can't change him and make everything all right.*
No matter how much you love him or how strongly you feel you have to help him, you aren't going to be able to fix it. A boy who abuses the girl he supposedly loves needs the help of objective, trained people who will confront him and help him take responsibility for his battering if he's ever going to change.

That means he will have to admit that he is abusing. The chances of your making him do that aren't good. The director of a men's program in Marin County, California, went into a high school and separated the boys and girls out of a group of dating couples. Once alone, a number of the girls admitted that violence was taking place in their relationships. Not a single boy did.[4]

If he doesn't own up to the fact that he's being abusive and seek help, nothing you do will significantly change his behavior. Even if he does, the counseling he needs to become a nonviolent person takes time—more time than you can afford to sacrifice as a young person.

Taking on his trouble as your own only hurts both of you. As long as you're there trying to make it all better, he doesn't have to hurt. He doesn't have to fix what's broken, because you're doing it all.

Instead, tell yourself—*don't*.

Don't risk your own life trying to help someone who's abusing you.

Don't cling to his good points and imagine yourself saving him.

Don't accept his abuse because he has problems.

Don't believe the promises that he'll stop abusing you. If he doesn't get help he can't just stop.

If you don't walk away from the relationship, the abuse becomes more frequent and more severe as time goes by. Part of the battering boy's problem is that he can never be satisfied. He can never get what he thinks he wants from his girl, yet he thinks he can't live without her. Everything he does is a means of getting control over her, from hitting her and putting her down to pleading with her to stay and promising never to do it again—to blaming her for making him do it.

So if you simply forgive and forget, you can expect more violence. In a recent letter to "Dear Abby," the mother of a battered teenage girl wrote:

> I read with horror the letter from "Worried Mom," whose 17-year-old daughter suffered repeated beatings by her boyfriend. A few years ago I, too, was a worried mom with the same problem. I pleaded with my beautiful blond-haired Laura to break up with her boyfriend, who had hit her with his fists and knocked out her front teeth. Once he rolled up her arm in a car window and drove off, dragging her down the street.
>
> I also learned that he went to her dorm at college and terrified her when he held her over three flights, threatening to drop her. This kind of abuse continued for two years. I begged her to quit seeing him, but she "loved" him.
>
> On May 31, 1984, my precious daughter was found dead in a field. She was killed by repeated blows to her head. The crime is still "unsolved" (insufficient evidence).

Abby's answer:

I would like to repeat some advice to all women who have tolerated, first, repeated verbal abuse from a lover, then a few punches, slaps, shoves, and finally a full-scale beating: if you think you can change him, forget it. First charge him with assault, then run as though your life depended upon it, because it does.[5]

You know now that it needs to be done. Let's see if we can help you figure out how.

Getting Out

First, get yourself in the right frame of mind. Remember these points:

- Your situation is serious or could be.
- The only way to deal with it is to meet it head-on.
- It's up to you to initiate that, because he isn't going to.
- It's okay to grieve—for him, for yourself, and for the relationship.
- You will be able to let go eventually and feel good again.
- You're going to learn from this experience, and then your next relationship will be better.

Second, don't try to go it alone if you don't think you can. Having at least one person to talk to is a must for most girls. The feeling that no one cares or will or can help you is a horrible one, and that isolation makes you cling even more to your relationship with your boyfriend. You need guidance and information in deciding to leave and how and when to do it; you need support in going through with it; you need sympathy when it's over.

Still, it can be degrading and humiliating and a real blow to your pride. It seems to be even harder for teens than for adult women. The San Francisco family violence project, which serves hundreds of adults every year, receives only about ten calls from teens in that same time period.[6] The San Francisco police juvenile division receives two calls a month from fourteen- to sixteen-year-olds reporting dating violence, but nine out of ten don't end up pressing charges.[7] That's tattling to the adult world! Only 7 percent of all abuse shelter clients are teenagers, partly because they think such programs are just for married women.[8] Even fear that the person you go to will say, "You brought it on yourself," or "Why did you stick around so long and put up with it?" can keep you from seeking the help you need.

Finding the *right* person is the key. The person to go to:

- is not someone to tell you what to do but someone to give you information and help you carry out the decisions you make;
- is someone who will treat you with respect and compassion;
- is someone you can trust not to blab your situation to everyone.

Your first impulse may be to turn to a friend your own age, and that's good for a start. Just be sure that friend meets the above criteria, and don't be surprised if he or she doesn't know what to say or just doesn't understand. Would you have, before it happened to you?

Chances are, though, you will appreciate some adult help, and although the older generation may seem like the enemy from time to time, some compassionate people *were* born before 1972! Take stock of whom you know who fits the bill: your family doctor, your clergyman, a teacher, counselor, or youth adviser, the parent of a friend, a relative, and possibly the wisest choice of all, your parents.

Except in extreme circumstances, your parents are the best people to tell. You need their help and support because you may have a long recovery process ahead of you. They can encourage you, help you feel good about yourself, make you feel loved as no one else can. Because they're with you on a day-to-day basis, they can help you regain your faith in the good side of life.

You may have a stack of reasons as tall as you are for not going to your parents, but hear me out.

You know for sure they'll blame you. "How could you let this happen? I told you to stop seeing him." In that case, having your counselor or a friend with you to help offset some of that is a good idea, but it's still your best bet to share it with them. They love you more than anyone does, and in the end they'll realize you're not at fault.

You're embarrassed, especially in the case of sexual assault. That's very real, but it isn't enough reason to deny yourself their help. Keeping in mind that it was a crime of violence, not of sex, will help.

It's a blow to your independence to run to them when you're in trouble. In the first place, it's just a temporary retreat, and besides, even adults want to be cuddled and comforted sometimes. It won't stop you from growing up!

You don't want to upset them. I'm a parent, so trust me: They'd be more upset knowing you were suffering and didn't tell them. It's in parents' contracts to be upset when their kids are upset!

You don't want them to find out what you were doing at the time of an attack. Maybe you were at his place when his parents were out of town instead of spending the night at your girlfriend's as you told them. Remember, just because you broke the rules doesn't mean you invited assault. Most parents will be more concerned about you and your welfare.

Your boyfriend threatened to hurt you if you told your parents. You'll need to decide for yourself whether he's really likely to carry out that threat. Then, to protect yourself even further, tell your parents about the *threat*, too.

You know they'll forbid you ever to see him again. You may know you have to break up with him but want to do it in your own good time. Explain that to them. Agree to let Dad sit in the car with the motor running while you talk to your boyfriend. If you have good reasons and share them calmly and rationally, most parents will see your point and be willing to help. If you can, at least give them the benefit of the doubt. You've never been in this situation before, so you really don't know how they're going to respond.

When and if you do share what's happened with your folks, it will help to be prepared for several different re-actions. Some parents will try to overprotect you and blame themselves. Reassure them. Some will withdraw a little out of shock and embarrassment, especially dads. Remind yourself why, and forgive them for that. A few will want to get back at the boy. Try to dissuade them from any more violence. You've had enough. Some may just be unable to understand at first. Give them this book to read.

If you absolutely cannot tell your parents or if you do and it doesn't help, you still have other options. These are available to you even in addition to their support if you think you need more specialized information. They include:

- shelters for battered women (which offer counseling, support services, and legal assistance in addi-

tion to shelter; there are 900 in the United States);
- family violence projects;
- mental health centers;
- crisis hotlines;
- peer counseling groups at your school.

If you're at a loss as to where to find any of these, look in
the phone book under *Crisis, Battered women, Family
violence,* or *Domestic violence,* or simply call the operator.
There are people out there who want to help you.

Remember, of course, that the help you get won't assist
you in making the relationship better. The boy needs help,
and he isn't going to get it with you there. To protect
yourself, sooner or later you have to say good-bye. How do
you do that? Try these guidelines put together by people
who work with abused women:

1. The time of an attack is not the time to break off
   the relationship. Don't argue or hit back. Get away
   from him as fast as you can until he has calmed
   down.
2. Once you're away from him, take time to think of
   how you want to handle the breakup. Don't hurry.
   Don't let anyone pressure you. Remember your
   rights and practice them.
3. Pick a safe time and place. Using the phone is
   not chicken. Writing a letter isn't a cop-out. *Your*
   safety comes first. You have no obligation ever to
   see him again. If you do, don't agree to a secluded,
   isolated environment. The middle of McDonald's
   with your support network two tables away is my
   suggestion.
4. Decide ahead of time what you want to say so you
   can be prepared for his answers. Communicate the

anger you've been covering up. Be specific about
the incidents that have led you to your decision.
Be honest. Don't give him false hopes. Don't be
physical (kissing him good-bye, etc.). Be cold,
aloof, and abrupt if you have to.

5. If you can't flat-out end the relationship, at least do
yourself this favor. Tell him you won't see him
until he has sought help for his problem. Then be
sure you stick to that. You're still taking a risk, but
at the same time you're telling him you won't put
up with violence, and that you're responsible only
for keeping yourself safe.

And if he doesn't take no for an answer? Tell someone—
right away. Get help in protecting yourself. Keep in mind
that every time your partner physically assaults you, he is
committing a crime and you have the option of filing a
criminal complaint. You are in charge of your own life.
Don't let *him* be!

Getting Better

Any kind of abuse, no matter how minor, can leave you
shaky inside and out. It will take time to heal. Let that be
okay and give yourself time. Here are some of the things
you can expect:

- *Still having feelings for him, and feeling stupid
  about having those feelings.* You can't turn them off
  like a light switch, and besides, anyone who has lost
  a love relationship needs time to grieve and heal. If
  you've been forced to be dependent for a long time,
  that makes it even harder. "You've given yourself

away," writes Jim Long, "and it's hard to take your-self back."[9]

- *Denying that it was as bad as you thought it was then.* It *was*! Denial is just part of the healing process.
- *Feeling angry with yourself because you did (or didn't do) things that in retrospect seem dumb or naive.* At the time they were natural reactions to a most unnatural situation.[10] Forgive yourself.
- *Going through some very depressing days.* In suffering abuse you've had a shock to your system. In breaking off your relationship you've endured a loss. You're definitely going to feel depressed, but it *will* pass. How long it takes varies from person to person. It can take from three months to a year.
- *Thinking that everything you've dreamed of about love has been shattered.* Maybe not everything. Through him you saw what you wanted for yourself. Now you can see that you can get it without him and that no one, boy or otherwise, is going to hand it to you. If you can grow from this painful situation (rather than hanging on to what might have been or what was), and if you can visualize yourself acting on your own real, true ideas from now on, everything isn't lost.
- *Wondering if you'll ever be able to love and trust a guy again.* You bet, because you've learned what *isn't* a healthy relationship, and you probably won't fall into that trap a second time. You have nothing but the best to look forward to. As Helen Benedict puts it, "comparing a violent relationship to a real relationship is like comparing a slug in the mouth to a kiss."[11]

Of course, all that takes more than just time. You'll need to do some work to turn the whole thing around.

Start by facing your fears about being without someone. You'll deal with them a lot faster that way and realize that you *can* get along without him so that you can get on with getting along with yourself. In fact, before you even think about getting into another relationship, it's a good idea to get to know and like you. Take the time to heal and to think about what you really need from a relationship.

Next, take care of yourself. Turn his old messages around and make them positive. Tell yourself, "I am a good person. I'm doing the best I can. I'm worth knowing and loving." Pursue some of the things you like to do. Pull out that tennis racket, those old Victorian novels, that paintbrush. Go out with the girls in a crazy, giggling group. Think about the fact that you've done what you know is right, and be proud of that. You are a person of value. Respect yourself.

Try working on the things that kept you in an abusive relationship, and get some help in this if you have to. Maybe you need to learn healthy ways to express anger. Perhaps you need to polish some communication skills or learn to be assertive. It may even be that you need to clear up some mistaken ideas about what a good relationship is. Whatever it is, it can help you heal from your hurt and insure that you'll never have to endure abuse again.

Clare, a sixteen-year-old who was battered by her boyfriend for several months, says it isn't easy to put it all behind you. "You know how people say you never forget your first love?" she says. "Well, this was my first love."[12]

No, it isn't easy, but it isn't impossible, and it's certainly worth doing. After all, there's only one you. You have to take a chance on you before anyone else will.[13] Maybe the words of someone who has been there will help you.

After a while you learn the subtle
difference between holding a hand and
chaining a soul
And you learn that love doesn't mean
leaning and company doesn't mean security
And you begin to learn that kisses aren't
contracts and presents aren't promises
After a while you learn that even sunshine
can burn if you get too much
So you plant your own garden and decorate
your own soul instead of waiting for
someone to bring you flowers[14]

CHAPTER 8

If You Batter

I f you have a problem with your violence and you've decided to read this chapter, you're a special kind of person. It's hard to admit you might have something inside that you haven't been able to control so far. And no matter what mistakes you may have made, there's a decent person in there, one who obviously wants to learn how to treat the people you love better, including yourself.

If you're like most guys in your position, you're frustrated, afraid, and confused. You want to get a handle on your anger, you want to get out of the trap of hitting and hurting, but you just don't know how. Reading this chapter can't change that all by itself, but it can give you a start. You can do three things right away to get you on the right track:

1. *Admit that you batter.*

It is considered *abusive* if:

- your girlfriend has shown she is afraid of you;
- you've broken things in her presence;
- you verbally harass her, especially when she disagrees with you;

- she can't get angry at you without your becoming *more* angry;
- you have used any kind of physical force with her— shoving, grabbing, anything;
- she's complained that you're trying to control her;
- she has broken up with you one or more times for mistreating her;
- you're afraid she'll break up with you for the way you treat her.

If any of the above applies to you, or if you can feel those tendencies and are afraid they'll get out of control, the first step in getting better is to say, "I am a batterer. I have chosen to use violence in my relationships. I can't blame it on alcohol or drugs. I can't blame it on the stress I'm under. I *choose* to abuse someone I care about."

Now that you've said it, you've won a big part of the battle. The possibility for violence is in every one of us, but we resort to it less if we admit it than if we deny it and say, "Not me, man!" or, "Hey, I just slapped her once. What's the big deal?"

2. *Realize you're not alone.*

You aren't the only one who hits and swears and pushes people around, nor are you rare, nor are you suffering from mental illness. Using violence in a relationship is something you've learned—you and half the men in America. Fifty percent of American men become violent with a woman at least once. Twenty percent are violent regularly, which means once a month or more. Three out of four men use verbal abuse as a mechanism of control in relationships.[1]

Just because you are in something of a majority doesn't mean it's okay, mind you. It's just helpful to know that you aren't alone with your problem. Many men have been there, and many have been helped and healed. You could be one of those.

3. *See that you can change—and that you should.*

The tendency to use violence in relationships only gets worse unless you do something about it. It almost never gets better all by itself. In fact, it escalates so much that if you hit, push, and shove your girlfriend now, it's almost guaranteed that you will inflict even more severe physical injuries on the women you date as you get older. You're also a likely candidate for being a wife-beater. That means you might break bones. Cause head injuries. Create scars. Raise a son who batters. Raise a daughter who accepts abuse. Wind up in jail. Ruin your own life and someone else's.

You know how impossible it is to change on your own if you've ever promised your girlfriend you'd never lay a hand on her in anger again. It didn't work, did it? That's because violence happens in a cycle, something like the diagram below.[2]

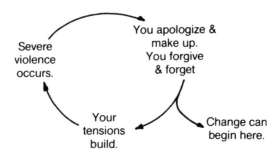

So how do you change? By facing up to all of the above, and then going to people who are trained to help you. You can't do it on your own, and that's okay. It doesn't make you any less of a man. Having the good sense and the desire to be better than you are makes you *more* of a man. Now read on, and see how.

Getting Help

As we've said, you can't lick this problem by yourself, and no book can help you totally either. You need human support because you have some heavy work ahead of you. You have to unlearn old behaviors and learn new ones, and if you could do that without help you'd have done it by now!

What we're talking about here is counseling. Don't panic! It doesn't have to be a psychiatrist or a psychologist. In fact, if you can work it out, it's preferable if it isn't just one person at all. Part of the reason you lash out is because you're isolated. Although you may have a lot of buddies, you probably don't talk to them about personal things, feelings, fears—and least of all your violence. With everything bottled up inside of you, it's no wonder you explode now and then. It isn't all right that you do, it's just no wonder.

The ideal counseling for you is a support *group*, preferably of guys who've been where you are and know the feelings, the angles, the excuses, and the heartache. Such groups *are* available. Until a few years ago domestic violence programs were largely for the female victims of battering, but many now have special programs for males— support groups where men can relax, talk about their anger and what to do about it, and realize their potential for being great guys. You learned to be the man you are in groups of men—scout troops, athletic teams. To learn to be a different kind of man, you need a group of men again, this time to sort things out with, not shoot the bull with; to talk truly with, not just brag to and try to keep up with, locker-room story for locker-room story. For the first time in your life, you could find yourself talking honestly with other men.

Most of these groups are led by trained men who can

guide you toward specific ways to manage your anger and get rid of violence in your life. They'll help you to:

1. avoid violence by recognizing your anger cues and taking time-outs;
2. relax and communicate clearly during conflicts;
3. let go of your need to control;
4. get past denial (just because you never put her in the hospital doesn't mean you aren't abusive), forget excuses, and assume responsibility for your own actions;
5. realize that it's okay to get angry, that it's using violence when you're angry that isn't okay;
6. find ways to get rid of stress, and react without violence to the stress you can't get rid of;
7. be the man you want to be instead of who you think you ought to be;
8. do good things for yourself;
9. break down your isolation and loneliness;
10. get ready for the next relationship and make it a healthy one;
11. accept people without trying to manipulate or change them;
12. examine your feelings;
13. control your inner turmoil instead of letting it control you.

Where to find people like that is your next step.

First look for domestic violence programs in the yellow pages of your phone book under Crisis Intervention Services or Social Service Agencies. It nothing turns up, try calling the Center for Women's Policy Studies (202-872-1770) or the National Council Against Domestic Violence (202-347-7015) for the men's program nearest you. If there isn't one in your area, try a women's crisis center for a recommendation. Community programs such as these usually require only what payment you can afford. Under no circumstances should you feel like a geek about calling because you're under age or aren't married. If the fear of being laughed at or turned down is keeping you from calling, have an adult friend do it. If someone does refuse you because of your age or situation, report them to the NCADV, whose number is given above.

If none of these avenues turns up anything for you, you might want to ask your folks about private counseling or go yourself to your community mental health center. Even a school counselor or a religious counselor you feel comfortable with can be helpful, and if they know nothing about the subject, have them read this book. One-on-one therapy is not as good as group counseling in your situation, but it's one hundred and fifty percent better than trying to go it alone. Just having someone who will listen to your fears and prevent you from falling back on your old excuses will be helpful.

If you have six months of good help and you're willing to work at it, you'll probably lick relationship violence. However, even at that, if you simply walk back into a world that says, "Bullshit! A woman needs a good rap in the mouth once in a while!", it could all go down the tubes again. Try to set up a lifelong maintenance support system for yourself. Surround yourself with honest, nonviolent people, adults as well as peers. Keep in touch with people who know about your problem and won't let you snowball them. Don't isolate yourself to one friend you're not honest with anyway. Once you've learned to own up to who you are and what you feel, keep it going. You owe it to yourself as well as to the women in your future.

Helping Yourself

Even when you get counseling, overcoming a problem like abusive behavior is going to take a lot of work by you personally. Below is a list of things you can do to make sure you'll never again lay a violent hand on someone you love.

1. *Break off your current relationship.*

It's going to take you a while to get a grip on things. Why risk hurting your girlfriend more or getting yourself into deeper trouble by sticking around? Even married couples usually separate while a husband is undergoing therapy for domestic violence. The two of you may have created a kind of third person out of your relationship, a composite of you both. Letting go of that can be like letting go of yourself. But when you do, you'll be forced to reexamine the real you, your own life, something you can't do when you're completely wrapped up in her. Besides, love flourishes best when you are the least dependent on it and withers when you desperately need it.[3] What you learn about yourself will help you find a relationship that blooms instead of dying on the vine next time.

2. *Work on managing your anger.*

There's a big difference between anger and violence. Anger is a healthy, normal emotion. Violence is an expression of anger with negative consequences. Anger itself isn't the problem. Everybody gets angry, and if they didn't we'd all be doormats. Violence is the problem because it makes you a slave to your anger. The secret is to find other ways to deal with anger when it inevitably rears its head. Trying to suppress it only leads to explosive outbursts (as you already may have found out!) These are suggestions made by counselors and therapists who know their stuff:

- Pay attention to the warning signals of anger. When you start to get mad, do you clench your fists, grit your teeth, get sick to your stomach? Do something as soon as you feel the first signs. Don't wait until it's too late.
- Just flat walk away when you're angry!
- Find somebody to talk to.
- Find a place to go and yell. Tell yourself why you're angry.
- Take immediate exercise (run, throw a ball against a wall, ride a bike as hard as you can).
- Write an unsent letter; write down your thoughts and then throw the paper away.

Those are the dos. These are the don'ts. When you're angry:

- Don't try to control her responses; just control your own; violence never changes another person's behavior.
- Don't stuff it away, thinking, "I shouldn't be angry," or "She's just trying to make me mad and it isn't going to work."
- Don't let it escalate by pointing fingers and placing blame and calling names; try to direct it by saying, "I feel angry because _____ and I'm going to go away until I'm ready to talk about it." (Then when you do come back to talk, talk only about the subject!)
- Don't feel you've failed because you feel anger; say to yourself, "I'm in control of myself. I just need some time to cool off."
- Don't assume that when *she's* angry, it's your fault.

- Don't assume that in an argument somebody has to win; people argue because people are different, not because one of them is right and the other is wrong.

One of Changing Men's most successful alternatives to an explosion is a "time-out." When you feel the signals inside you, they say, leave the situation for one hour, and tell your partner that's what you're doing. Don't drink or drive. Do walk, run, or get some other kind of exercise. Breathe deeply until your muscles relax. At the end of one hour, go back and talk things out.

That's hard, because you've probably been taught that only a coward walks away from a fight. Darn it, you want control! You've got to have the last word! And what if she's gone when you get back? Yeah, it's tough. But it's worth it to let all that go and get the control you really need—over yourself. Nothing is worth getting violent over, and nobody "makes" you do anything.

3. *Build your self-esteem.*

You don't have to admit it to anyone but yourself, but isn't this true: you may be domineering, blustering, and self-advertising on the outside, but aren't you pretty fragile and afraid on the inside? A number of different things probably went to work on you early in life to make you that way, but the point now is that, although you may apologize for being abusive, you can't do anything about it as long as you feel terrible as a person.

Maybe you've abused your girlfriend out of jealousy. Isn't jealousy caused by your own self-doubts?

Maybe you really feel like a creep because of the way you've treated her. Doesn't all that remorse and heavy, negative stuff make it hard for you to cooperate?

Maybe you put yourself down a lot because of the things

you've done. Doesn't that make it that much easier to put everyone else down, too?

Maybe you feel pretty much like a nobody. Doesn't that make you want to prove yourself somehow, perhaps by getting control in your relationship?

Just about everyone is struggling in some way to build or protect self-esteem, because that's a very positive need. A person whose self-esteem is low and whose self-doubt is high can't live that way for long without trying to get some significance somehow. Hitting may be one way of doing that.

So it's a cinch that if you could build up your own image of yourself you wouldn't feel you had to hit or yell or shove around people who are smaller and more vulnerable than you. The way you feel about yourself parallels your attitudes toward other people. If you start treating yourself better, you'll do the same for the people you love.

So be nice to yourself, guy! If you have to, make a list of the things you really get satisfaction out of doing and do them.

Get to know your own good qualities. Again, take pen in hand and write out the things you really like about yourself. Keep the list handy. Look at it—*often.*

Pat yourself on the back for trying to get rid of your less-than-desirable behaviors. That alone makes you a much better than average human being. You're all right. Know it!

4. *Work on dealing with stress.*

Stress, like politics, pollution, and the Internal Revenue Service, is here to stay in today's high-pressure world. It'll be worth your while to learn how to keep it at a minimum now. Your brain is under your control. You can decide how you'll function. Leaving it to chance or impulse means giving up the right to use your own self for your own good. Man, you don't want to do that! So:

- Quiet yourself down when you feel stressed; imagine a nice place (a Hawaiian island will do!) and put yourself mentally there.
- *Relax*; one simple exercise is to sit quietly in a straight-backed chair or lie on the floor, concentrate on your breathing, and be aware of each breath as it enters and leaves. Do that for ten minutes twice a day, and you'll have stress on a leash.
- When you start to get stressed, ask yourself why. If you need to, talk to somebody about what's bothering you; then sit down and decide what, if anything, you can constructively do about it and do it. After all, stress comes largely from feeling that you can't do anything about your problems; you might not get control over everything, but there's a lot you can overcome.
- Anger may be the only emotion you've been willing to pay attention to until now; pay attention to other things you feel—it's okay. You have a right to your feelings. They don't make you a wimp.
- If you're not getting what you really want and need in a relationship, ask for it in a way that isn't demanding or hostile; you do have that right.
- If you don't want to do something, just say no.
- Try to be realistic about your goals; you aren't going to be perfect, so don't push yourself beyond reasonable limits.
- Keep your problems in perspective; no one event is going to determine the rest of your life. Your grades aren't good enough for the Academy? Look around for another career alternative. Your girlfriend is

going to break up with you? She's a teenager! It's in her contract to shop around! There are other girls—after you get over this one.

- Be sure your schedule allows time to relax and time to exercise and time for your friendships.
- Find an adult you can talk to—about anything. We can *all* use that.

5. *Eliminate the need for power over.*

Power *with* another person, now that's good stuff. You and a partner can have the world if you work together. But power *over*? It never works. It's bad news. Let go of it.

Letting go isn't surrender to an enemy. A relationship shouldn't be a competition where somebody always has to win and it had better be you! Even when there's conflict, and there will be, it can be cooperative conflict. You can come up with a solution that's good for both of you. But get rid of that win-lose stuff that's in everything else from football to the work world. It doesn't belong in love. David Seabury wrote in *The Art of Selfishness*, "Put love in prison and it dies. Restrict it and it turns to hate. Force it and it disappears."[4]

As an abuser, aren't you locked into only one way of dealing with the frustrations in your life? Aren't you taking that out on somebody who may not even be responsible for your stress? Okay, so you feel powerless with parents, teachers, principals, coaches, and cops all in your face. But you aren't completely without control. Instead of trying to get power over her and everybody else, turn it to yourself. You're the sculptor of your life and your well-being. Do what you can about your own life now, and let her work on hers.

6. *Learn your sexual responsibilities.*

The word "responsibility" may sound like something

that should only go along with taking out the garbage and getting your homework done, but it isn't just a burden or a duty. It's an *ability*—an ability to *respond* to situations in a mature way. Sex is great, but it's something that takes place between *two* people. Your responsibility is to respond to sexual situations with the other person in mind as well as yourself. If you've been sexually abusive, these are the things you'll need to start learning:

- To consider the feelings of your partner as well as your own.
- To show respect for those feelings (no fair saying stuff like, "Don't be a prude").
- To realize that sex should be a *mutual* pleasure—and never a punishment.
- To realize that pressure doesn't create desire when there was none before; if she doesn't want to, *she doesn't want to*, and you can't make her want to.
- To realize that forced sex isn't really sex; it's a violent crime.
- To learn to recognize the words and actions from a girl that mean *"No!"*
  "I don't feel like it."
  "I'm not ready."
  "I don't know."
  "Please!"
  "I'm confused."
  "Let's take our time."
  "I don't like this."
  "I don't feel good about this."
  "That's enough."

Looking down.
Crying.

Cringing.
Moving away.
Avoiding being alone.[5]

If You're Afraid You May Become a Batterer

If you've been reading this chapter looking for something that can help you control the frightening violent tendencies you've felt but haven't succumbed to yet, you've come to the right place. Abuse is easier to prevent than it is to stop.

First of all, these are the warning signs. If you have several of these characteristics, you have reason for concern.

- You're very jealous.
- You sulk silently when you're upset.
- You have an explosive, unpredictable temper.
- You criticize and put your girlfriend down often.
- You have trouble expressing your feelings—any of them.
- You drink heavily or use drugs.
- You hold women in contempt and believe it's the male role to be in charge.
- You're protective of your girlfriend to the point of controlling her every move—her behavior, her money, her decisions; you're anxious when she doesn't spend all her free time with you or doesn't follow your advice.
- You were physically or emotionally abused by your parents.
- Your dad abuses his wife.
- You display violence against people other than your girlfriend.
- You commit violent acts against objects or animals.

- You sometimes feel as if you're two different people, sort of a Dr. Jekyll–Mr. Hyde.

If that list describes you somewhat, you can follow the advice given for a batterer and benefit from it. See a counselor. Join a support group. It doesn't matter if you've never actually slapped or shoved or raped your girlfriend. If you're afraid you might, it's worth looking into.

If There's Violence in Your Family

If you've been raised with cussing, screaming, beating, constant putting-down, you're more at risk for relationship abuse. Thousands of reinforcements throughout your life have told you it's okay to treat people you love that way. Overcoming that is almost as hard as changing your name or the color of your eyes.

But Terry Davidson, daughter of a wife-beater and author of the book *Conjugal Crime*, says this: "The statistics say you may be doomed to repeat the pattern of your parents. I say you can rise above it, and respect women, men, and yourself."[6]

It will take work from you and help from someone who understands where you're coming from. But here's what you can do to get started:

- Make plans for your future. You don't have to live at home forever. Consciously work out a life plan that doesn't include violence.
- Find a substitute family. That doesn't mean abandon your own. Just find a family, perhaps that of one of your friends, where you can spend some time and see how a nonviolent home operates.
- Develop your independence. The sooner you can

live your own life, the easier it will be to break old habits.

- Appreciate the good things in your life. That will keep your self-esteem up.
- Find interests that will make you feel proud of yourself.
- If there's a male adult you really admire, make friends with him. He'll serve as a nonviolent role model. You can silently learn from him what it is to be a man who doesn't hit.
- Get some counseling. You'll need help in learning ways other than violent ones for expressing your feelings.

Above all, don't let the past smother you. What matters now is the present and the future. Admit now that abuse is a problem for you. Decide now that you want to change that. Get yourself some help now to turn things around.

It will make the future a whole different ball game.

CHAPTER ◇ 9

Helping a Friend Who's in a Violent Relationship

Ardis came off the bench and grabbed the sweater I was about to pull over my head. Bunching it under her arm, she took hold of my left elbow and showed me the bruise there like it was Exhibit A.

"Don't try to tell me Kyle didn't do this to you, because I know."

I didn't say anything.

She pulled her eyes close together. "Okay, fine. But I'm going to tell *you* something. Even if you don't care about yourself, I care about you. Break up with him, Holly."

Woodenly I took my sweater from her and slid it over my head, the shame oozing through the threads. "I'm going to—eventually."

"When? Tonight?"

"I don't know."

"Are you afraid?"

"I don't know."

"I'll be there with you if you want. I'll tell him for you. He wouldn't even think about trying to punch *me* out."

"Ardie, just leave me alone!"

There was a sudden silence in the locker room. She rotated her shoulders in an effort at self-control. "You don't have to scream at me. I'm just trying to help you."

"I told you before. Telling me to break up with Kyle isn't helping me. I don't want to break up with him yet. I want to help him."

"You have lost it. You can't help a guy like Kyle. He's a loser."

I didn't answer. I just stared down at the hem of my sweater until she got up and left.[1]

"Ever since you started going out with Holly it's like you've got something rammed up your backside every minute," Drew said. "You were laid *back* before, compared to the way you are now."

Sigmund Freud is resurrected.

"She's too possessive."

Ah—Dr. Joyce Brothers.

"It's not like it was at the start. You guys don't have fun. Everytime I see you, you're either having another fight or she's biting on your ear trying to get you to make up from one."

Enter Dr. Ruth.

It was probably a full minute before I realized he was just looking at me. I said, "What?"

"I can't figure it out. Why do you stay around a

chick you fight with all the time?"

"Everybody fights. You can't say you and Sandy don't fight."

He raised both dust-colored eyebrows. "Yeah, I can. We've had one argument."

I snickered nervously. "And then you smacked her once and it was okay, huh?"

"Yeah, right, knocked her right up the side of the head."

I laughed out loud.

"Hey, Weiser, man, are you serious?" he said.

"About what? Would you quit asking so damn many questions?"

"About smacking her."

"Lighten up." I set my Coke down a little too heavily on the table. The edges of everything were getting fuzzy and it was all I could do to keep them in the lines, keep my stomach from heaving its contents all over the kitchen, and keep my eyes from betraying the terror that was crawling up my insides.

"We've had some bad fights, okay, and right now it's the pits because I just blew up at her the other day and I can't even take her out and make it up to her because my father's taking every one of my paychecks."

I stopped. Drew was looking hard at me. "Something is screwed," he said. "Holly's not good for you, man. Why don't you drop her?"

When the kitchen stopped reeling, I just shook my head. "I can't, man," I said.[2]

Ardis, Drew, Holly, and Kyle are characters from a book, but although their names and actual situations are fictitious, their personalities and reactions are based very tightly on real people caught in the web of dating violence. Drew and Ardis, like friends in real life, are almost as frustrated and angry as the victim and her boyfriend. If you have a friend who's on either the giving or the receiving end of a violent relationship and you've tried to help in some way, then you know: It's probably one of the toughest things going.

Maybe you were told you were imagining things, that it really wasn't as bad as it looked.

Maybe you were told you were interfering and to mind your own business!

Maybe your advice was taken—for a while—and then the two of them got right back together again and started the entire mess all over.

Maybe your friendship was splintered because of it.

If you received any of those reactions, nobody would blame you if you gave up trying. Who can help somebody who doesn't want to be helped, right?

That would be true, except that most people involved in an abusive situation do want help. It just has to be the right kind of help, and that *can* come from you. Here's how.

Get into the Right Frame of Mind Yourself First

It's so easy to stand outside a violent relationship and say, "Well, for Pete's sake, if you'd just do this, this and this, your problems would be over!" Don't fall into that mode. Instead, try to get your head in this place before you say anything:

First, don't place blame anywhere, but particularly not on the person being abused. It's tempting to do that, especially if you're a girl, too. You see a girl being hurt by a boyfriend, you think, "Could that happen to me?", and then you soothe your own fears by thinking, "Nah. I'm not like her, so I'm not in danger." Just because blaming the victim makes you feel safer, as if you have more control than she does, doesn't mean it's going to help *her*. She's not responsible for someone else's choice to use violence. She has enough shame to deal with. Don't pile more on.

Second, don't accept any of the stereoptypical myths about abuse (He must really love you if he gets mad enough to hit you; She must be provoking you to do it somehow; If you're staying, you must like it, etc.). If you need to, go back and review Chapter 3. That's part of how these kids got into this mess in the first place! Don't perpetuate the problem.

Know What You Can Do to Help a Battered Girl— And What You Can't

What you *can't* do is force her to leave, force her to get help, or force her to listen to and heed your advice, no matter how sound it may be. You can't assume that you know what's best for her because you're not she. Whatever she does has to be her decision, or it won't stick.

What you *can* do is this:

1. Know where she can go for help (see Chapter 7) and have names and phone numbers ready. Offer to go with her or be there while she makes a phone call. Then wait patiently, because she has to be ready.
2. Let her talk and just listen and *believe* her. You may hear one of three things: (a) she thinks this is the way it's always going to be, and she wants find a way to simply deal with it; (b) she wants to try to

change him; (c) she wants to try to change herself. Some of that will be hard to listen to, but chances are deep down she knows what she has to do. She just needs someone supportive to hear her, give her problem some significance, tell her she has courage, and let her make her own decision. She needs that kind of confidence.

3. Assure her of confidentiality, and don't tell anyone else unless you first tell her that you're going to. Don't try to talk to her boyfriend about it. That only spells more trouble for her.

4. Remember that getting out of the relationship is essential, so don't encourage her to work it out with the guy. At the same time don't, like Ardis, tell her point-blank that she's stupid if she doesn't get out. She has to reach that conclusion and make the move on her own.

5. Be there. Be part of her support system. Encourage her to talk to an adult she trusts.

6. Understand her, but don't study her. Don't try to help her figure out what it is about her that lets guys abuse her. In the first place. it's her abuser who needs to be analyzed, not she, and that kind of approach only adds to her guilt.

7. If you are witness to or see the results of serious physical injury, don't be afraid to involve an adult or even the police. That's not being a traitor. That's possibly saving a friend. If you watch your friend being choked or see her with a broken jaw, that's the time for you to take action, no matter what she says.

8. Don't take it personally if she refuses your help. While you have a responsibility to do all you can,

the decision is ultimately hers. You can't "save" her. You can only let your offer stand: "I'll be here whenever you want my help." It's important to say that, out loud, just as it's important to say, "I won't get mad if you don't break up with him. I'll be here for you." Don't leave her with no one to turn to when she does decide it's time.

9. If you suspect she's being abused but she doesn't come to you, it's okay to go to her and open some doors, which may be just what she's waiting for. Try referring to it—"Is Jeff treating you okay?" Give her a chance to gracefully say whether she wants to confide in you or not—"It sounds as if it's hard for you to talk about." Let her know you're available and concerned—"Is it something you feel like talking about to me?" Again, however, don't push. If she knows you're there, chances are she'll come to you when the time is right for *her*.

Know What You Can Do to Help a Boy Who Batters— And What You Can't Do

It's a lot harder to help a guy who batters than the girl he's battering because of denial.

He may deny he's hurting her at all. She's lying, he may tell you. You know women will use every trick in the book to get to you.

He may deny it's as bad as she says it is. Come on, he just called her a name, grabbed her by the arm, gave her a little push. You know how girls get hysterical and exaggerate.

He may admit he's smacking his girlfriend and calling her a slut on a regular basis, but he may not think he needs help for that because, come on, that's the way guys are. It's okay to keep your woman in line, no matter what you have to do.

It's important to know that's what you're up against when you approach a friend who's bullying his girlfriend. It will then follow that you can't *force* him to do anything—admit he's wrong, break up with the girl, change his ways. So what *can* you do?

1. Confront him with what he's doing, and give him your opinion of it. Peer pressure, as you know, is pretty strong stuff. If you're a friend he respects, he may listen.
2. Then, again, he may not. If he comes back with a mouthful of excuses, refuse to accept them. If he rationalizes his behavior, call him on it. If he falls back on the myths, expose them as such. Don't let him talk himself, or you, into letting battering be okay.
3. Realizing that you are not equipped to give him the kind of help that will change him for life, be prepared to tell him where he *can* get it. (See Chapter 8). Offer to go with him or be there when he calls. Don't push him. Just make it easier for him to do it himself.
4. Knowing the seriousness of the situation, encourage him to talk to an adult friend he trusts. Don't take on yourself the entire burden of responsibility for keeping Chuck from breaking Shannon's nose. A strong, understanding adult needs to know what's going on.
5. Although you won't be helping him if you accept what he's doing, you will be if you accept *him*. Care about him, and let him know you care. Point out his strong points. Let him know you don't think

he's a total loser. He may not show it, but chances are his self-esteem has hit rock bottom. You can help there.

6. Be prepared to lose his friendship, at least for a while. Nobody wants to be told they're screwing up royally, and a lot of people will respond to that by tossing you right out of their lives. Know going in that that could happen, and decide whether you're going to say, "Fine. That's the end of it then," or "I'll still be here when you need me, pal." But don't think for a minute that if the friendship ends over this issue, it was your fault. It may take a number of shattered relationships of all kinds for your buddy to realize he needs to change.

Watching friends hurt and be hurt is definitely no fun. It's natural to want to help, and it's good to try to offer the right kind of help. That not only says something pretty fine about you, but it's a step toward stopping the web of domestic violence that continues to grow. So even if your efforts seem to have no positive results, hang in there. Maybe what you do will at least plant a seed that'll sprout later on. You can never tell—and it sure doesn't hurt to try.

CHAPTER ◇ 10

Putting a Stop to Relationship Violence

A long with the good stuff—computers, civil rights, the polio vaccine—the generations before you have also left you some trash, not the least of which is domestic violence in epidemic proportions. You live in a society where you have a fifty-fifty chance of marrying someone who will abuse you, or whom you will abuse. A society where wife-beating and child abuse are handed down like a legacy. Where violence and sex are blithely linked in the media. Where kids grow up learning it's okay to degrade and molest and beat someone up in the name of love.

Yet there *is* so much "good stuff" in our society that it's easy to take the bad with the good and let the trash continue to pile up. Nobody really wants it there. They just tend to accept it as a pile that has always been there and probably always will be.

You don't have to do that. If you want to be an adult in a place where it isn't okay to beat your wife, abuse your kids, humiliate your girlfriend, and show it all on the screen as entertainment, you can help in the fight that's already going on to create a violence-free world.

You're one person, but your attitude and the action you take now *can* make a difference. Every cause—from the American Revolution to women's suffrage—was fought by individuals like you who said, "I don't want to live like this anymore."

Here's what you can do.

In Your Personal Life

1. Know what a healthy relationship is. Maybe you've never been slapped in the face or have never pushed a girl down stairs, but you still may not be aware of what an unhealthy partnership is and how it can lead to abuse. An example comes from a letter written by a seventeen-year-old girl to a teen magazine advice column.

> My boyfriend and I are both 17, and we love each other so much. The trouble is, he treats me like a prisoner! He limits the time I spend with my friends, then tells me what time I have to be home. Help!
>
> Worried in Wisconsin

> Dear Worried:
> If you feel your boyfriend's a jailer, remember you have the key! Unlock yourself from this losing situation by telling your guy that just because he loves you, he doesn't own you. Then explain you won't be asking his

permission to do things anymore. Reassure him that you want the relationship to work, but that it can't if he doesn't give you the room to be a well-rounded person.

You have the key. If you realize that a relationship like "Worried's" isn't a healthy one, no matter how intimate and romantic it may seem, you're taking a step toward eliminating abuse, at least in your own life.

Your current relationships are important. Dating is the process for practicing marriage, for working out what it means to care and be cared for, to set standards for yourself that will later be the foundation for permanent partnership. Now is the time to learn what's good about that, and what isn't.

A healthy relationship has these qualities:

- It's basically calm, rather than frantic.
- It's a friendship as well as a physical attraction.
- It accepts the need for privacy on both sides.
- It allows for differences of opinion.
- It doesn't force anybody to make a commitment or declare their undying love and devotion before they're ready to.
- It allows the time two people need to get to know each other and find out how compatible they are.
- It involves two people who already feel good about themselves and who carry those good feelings over into their relationship.
- It won't destroy them if they break up.
- It allows for the equal sharing of power and control— neither one dominates, neither one constantly submits.

- It doesn't make unrealistic demands on either partner.
- It involves no ideal expectations, no stereotypes; it involves two people of *different* sexes, not *opposite* sexes.[1]

Once again, Jim Long is right on in his summary of this issue:

"We must rediscover the simple word 'love.' What it is. What it isn't.

If it screams 'Mine!' it isn't love. If it broils with jealousy, it isn't love. If it celebrates wrong, it isn't love. If it can't wait, it isn't love. If it is violent—abusive—it isn't love.

We must rediscover the simple word 'love.' And never settle for less."[2]

A healthy relationship is simply one in which two people know and respect each other and have taken the time to make a history together. Otherwise there's only domination and possessiveness. Otherwise the groundwork is laid for abuse.

2. Know what you want in a relationship, and don't settle for anything less. That doesn't mean set up the unreal expectation that you're going to find Mr. or Ms. Perfect and live happily ever after. It does mean having respect for your own feelings and values and then thinking through what you really need and want in order to be happy with another person—and what you absolutely cannot and will not live with. Then stick to it. You have that right.

If you decide now that you want a woman who doesn't nag, gives you space to pursue sports and hobbies, and likes to cuddle, don't get into a steady relationship with a girl who is constantly jacking her jaws in your ear, pouts when you go to basketball practice, and gives you the cold shoulder everytime you reach for her—and expect to change her into what you want her to be. Your frustration will build, your anger will mount, and the choice to lash out will become pretty attractive. Don't figure this is the only girl who will ever look at you. Find one who doesn't get on your case and will go do her thing while you do yours.

Although it may seem that marriage and kids and career and life-style are light-years away at the moment, it isn't too early to consider how you feel about all that. We're talking about eliminating violence in the future—your future. You want an absorbing career? You want to devote yourself to your job and have a sophisticated life-style for a while after you're out of college? Know that. Date whomever you want. But don't marry a guy who is already talking kids and a ranch house in the country and chickens in the backyard. Remember Whistler, the artist who painted the famous "Whistler's Mother"? He said a great painting is made by knowing what not to put on a canvas. By the same token, successful living depends on knowing what not to put on your canvas, by knowing what to say no to.[3]

Learn Healthy Ways to Deal with Stress and Conflict

Schools in southern California teach a course called Skills for Violence-Free Relationships. Their philosophy is that if young people learn to recognize their feelings and develop healthy ways to handle daily stress as well as stressful life events, they are less likely to hurt other people. They devote an entire semester to it, so we can't possibly present it all here, but hitting some of the highlights can give you a start.

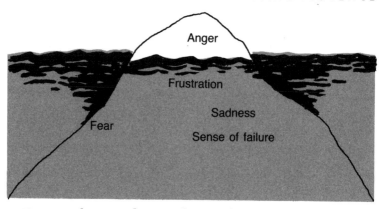

First on the agenda is understanding the stress feelings. They're like an iceberg. Only the tip, which is the anger, shows. The dangerous part, of both the iceberg and stress, is the part below the surface—the fear, the sadness, the frustration, and the sense of failure. If you let that stuff build up underneath, you're liable to plow right into somebody.[4]

What can be done instead of iceberging? Communicate your feelings in a nonblaming, nonattacking way. Let people know how you feel, how what they do affects you, and what you want them to do. Violence and communication can't exist together. If you are communicating clearly, there will be no room for violence.

Next, the course suggests looking at the way you currently cope with stress. If it's hurting you or someone else, it's not only unhealthy, but it isn't doing anything to eliminate the tension and in fact is just creating more. This is a good time to examine your coping strategies, because your old ways of dealing with the heavies may recently have been taken away from you, leaving you with nothing to replace them. Maybe you always cried when you were stressed as a kid, and now your parents or peers are telling you, "I don't care how much better that makes you feel, it's time to grow up and quit bawling everytime the going gets a little tough." If you need some suggestions to get you started, read Chapter 8 again.

The course also teaches conflict resolution skills, since conflict creates stress. Conflict is natural in relationships, but it's tough to handle because it causes anxiety and fear. Abuse is a way of reducing anxiety temporarily, but it makes for more problems rather than solving the ones that were already there.

You can use one of two strategies in a confrontation. You can go for the power strategy, the win-lose approach. That means using physical force, bribery, punishment, whatever it takes to make sure that you win and the other person loses. Or you can try a negotiation strategy, where you try to find a mutually satisfying solution. A negotiation strategy relies on equal power, not one person exerting power over another person.

The negotiation strategy requires some special skills. You have to be able to recognize a conflict when it comes up and figure out what it's all about. Then you have to be willing to initiate a confrontation on the subject and do it without putting the other person on the defensive or causing a major explosion. Once it's out in the open, you need to be able to listen to the other person's point of view and use problem-solving processes to arrive at a solution that's right for both of you. It's simple. So is the theory of relativity. No, it isn't easy, but you can learn to be assertive and problem-solve. It sure beats slamming or being slammed against a wall.

The Violence-Free curriculum teaches what communication stoppers are, those things that get in the way of all of the above. Try to avoid:

- interrupting,
- verbally attacking,

- dominating the conversation,
- judging the other person in the process,
- putting words into the other person's mouth,
- passing out put-downs and sarcastic remarks.

Even if you're assertive, that doesn't mean you can control the other person or that things will automatically go your way. But it does open communication and give you more choices. It keeps you from saying yes when you want to say no. When used properly at the right time, it will certainly keep you from abusing or being abused.

In Your World

Okay, so you're not the march-on-Washington, write-to-your-congressman type. But there are a couple of things you can do as an individual to make that small but important difference in the amount of violence that goes on around you.

1. Don't let battering be okay for your generation. Violence isn't genetic or instinctive; it's learned behavior, and any learned behavior can be unlearned. Call your friends on it when they start reflecting a machismo image. Do you sit around as a group, girls putting boys down, guys talking negatively about girls and "grading" them? Stop it. Show shock when people talk or exhibit brutality of any kind. Know the facts about battering that we've talked about here, and challenge your friends when they toss out stereotyped clichés (Women like to be hit, A guy has to keep a girl in line, etc.) Don't let people get away with linking hitting or being hit with being a "man" or a "woman" without letting them know they're still living in the dark ages. Don't be afraid to speak out. You can do more in a single conversation to change the attitudes of

your peers than any adult trying to drive it home for an entire semester.

2. Don't tolerate violence in the media. We've become desensitized by slice-and-dice movies in our society, and that's dangerous. Studies show that aggressive behavior is much more likely than normal following exposure to violence in any form, including on a screen.[5] The more violence you observe, the more tolerant you become of violent behavior. Change the channel when somebody's being beaten to a pulp on "McGyver." Refuse to go when your friends are taking off for a movie where a rape is the main event. Bad-mouth rock videos that depict women in chains with whips hanging nearby. If people don't expect and accept violence, they're not likely to commit it. Don't let it become accepted and expected in your own living room. Jim Long writes: "We don't have to get our values from TV, movies, and sleazy music. We know the value of love, kindness, and respect. Let's follow them. We can. We are that strong."[6]

3. Ask that antiviolence instruction be given in your school. *Everybody* has to be educated about battering, not just those already in the situation or those at risk. People are much better off if they never have to encounter it, because each time a person uses or experiences violence, the next time it becomes easier to use or easier to accept.[7] If you've read this book, you've seen the need. Now do what you can to pass it on. Short of marching into the principal's office and saying, "Look, guy, we need an antiviolence seminar" (which isn't a bad approach, really), you can go to health, home ec., or life studies teachers, student council officers, p.e. coaches, or the P.T.A. Many community domestic violence programs have people on their staffs who will visit high schools and junior highs with slide presentations, videos, and printed materials and tell

it like it is. Should you be brave enough (and if you are, more power to you) to put together your own program, the list of available audiovisual aids at the end of this chapter should be helpful to you. Learning to live peaceably in society is part of education. If you and your peers aren't getting that part in school, do someting about it.

4. Ask that help for teens be offered by your local domestic violence programs. One of the problems we've touched on in this book is the lack of aid for kids touched by relationship violence. A quick phone call to your local women's crisis center should tell you whether help for victims and perpetrators of teen dating violence is available in your area. If it isn't, offer to send them this book. Tell them about the videos and curricula that are now on the market. Ask them if they're willing to talk to teens who call in with abuse problems. Let them know there's a need. With their limited funds, no organization will set aside time and money for dealing with a problem they're not sure exists.

Enid Lloyd Keljik, a coordinator of the New York NOW's Task Force on the Battered Wife, wrote, "Both battered and batterer are victims of social ills they did not make and surely cannot cure, at least not alone."[8] Even if you're as young as thirteen or fourteen, you're part of society. You're responsible for its future. You can help cure its ills. Armed with the facts, the right attitude, and the drive to change things, you *can* help. If the trash pile is going to be carted away in your lifetime, you have to be there with a wheelbarrow.

AVAILABLE MATERIALS ON DATING VIOLENCE

"My Girl"
One-hour video on battering in teen relationships
    with curriculum guide
Rental fee $35
Battered Women's Alternatives
P.O. Box 6406
Concord, CA   94524
(415)676-2845

"When the Good Times Go Bad: Teen Age Dating
    Violence"
Twenty-five-minute video on high school dating vio-
    lence plus written manual with exercises in pass-out
    form
Rental fee $50
Turning Point
P.O. Box 103
Columbus, IN   47202
(812)379-9844

"Broken Dreams: The Secret of Dating Violence"
Slide show and discussion guide
Purchase price $100
The Women's Coalition of Duluth
(218)728-6481

"Power of Choice"
Thirty-minute video with teaching guide (includes
    topic of intervention by a friend)
Domestic Abuse Project
2445 Park Avenue South

Minneapolis, MN   55404
A school curriculum is also available.

"Skills For Violence-Free Relationships"
Secondary school curriculum
$27.50 per copy
Southern California Coalition on Battered Women
P.O. Box 5036
Santa Monica, CA   90405
(213)392-9874

"Dating Violence Can Break More Than Your Heart!"
Program implemented by Michigan Coalition Against
   Domestic Violence
P.O. Box 7032
Huntington Woods, MI   48070
(313)961-0290

"Acquaintance Rape: Awareness and Prevention for
   Teenagers"
"Macho: Is That What I Really Want?"
Booklets published by Alternatives to Fear
2811 East Madison, Suite #208
Seattle, WA   98112
$4 each, plus postage

For additional information, contact the National Coalition
Against Domestic Violence, 1-800-333-SAFE.

Chapter Notes

Chapter 1

[1] Jean Doss, Community Outreach Coordinator, Committee to Aid Abused Women, Sparks, Nevada, July, 1985.

[2] Don Conway-Long, Changing Men, St. Louis, Missouri, June 29, 1988.

[3] Susan Zakin, "Young Love, Violent Love," (San Francisco *Chronicle*, Jan. 14, 1986), p.16.

[4] Lisa Morrell, "Violence in Premarital Relationships," (*Response*, Fall, 1984), p.17.

[5] Claudette McShane, "Date Abuse: When Relationships Go Bad." (*Campus Life*, November 1985), p.35.

[6] Elizabeth Rodgers, "Sex and Your Body: Date Rape," (*Seventeen*, March, 1983), p.36.

[7] Conway-Long.

[8] Lenore Walker, *The Battered Woman* (New York: Harper & Row, 1979), p.192.

[9] Hans Toch, *Violent Men* (Chicago: Aldine Publishing Co., 1969), p.1.

[10] Federal Bureau of Justice, quoted in "Brawl in the Family," (*Science News*, May 5, 1984), p.287.

[11] Dr. Steinmetz, quoted by Roger Langley and Richard C. Levy in *Wife-Beating: The Silent Crisis* (New York: E.P. Dutton, 1977), p.2.

[12] Dr. Richard Gelles, quoted by Langley and Levy, p.3.

[13] Langley and Levy, p.9.

[14] Claire Safran, "Why Men Hate the Women They Love," (*Reader's Digest*, January, 1986), p.77.

[15] Barrie Levy, *Skills For Violence-Free Relationships* (South-

ern California Coalition on Battered Women, 1984), p.13.

[16] *Ibid*, p.11.

[17] Landley and Levy, p.5.

[18] *Ibid.*

[19] James Koval, quoted by Andrea Sachs, "Swinging—and Ducking—Singles" (*Time*, September 5, 1988), p.54.

Chapter 2

[1] Barrie Levy, *Skills for Violence-Free Relationships* (Southern California Coalition on Battered Women, 1984), p.7.

[2] *Ibid.*

[3] Helen Benedict, *Safe Strong, and Streetwise* (Boston: Little, Brown and Co., 1987), p.10.

[4] Jim Long, et al., "Date Rape," (*Campus Life*, December, 1985), p.44.

[5] Leslie Cantrell, *Into the Light* (Edmonds, WA: Chas. Franklin Press, 7821 175th Street SW, 1986), p.3.

Chapter 3

[1] Roger Langley and Richard Levy, *Wife-Beating: The Silent Crisis* (New York: E.P. Dutton, 1977), p.8.

[2] William A. Stacey and Anson Shupe, *The Family Secret* (Boston: Beacon Press, 1983),p.104.

[3] Esther Lee Olson, *No Place to Hide* (Wheaton, IL: Tyndale House Publishers, 1985), p.30.

[4] Leslie Cantrell, *Into the Light* (Edmonds, WA: Chas. Franklin Press, 1986), p.7.

[5] *Ibid.*

Chapter 4

[1] Hans Toch, *Violent Men* (Chicago: Aldine Publishing Co., 1969), p.137.

[2] David and Brannon, *The Forty-nine Percent Majority: The Male Sex Role,* quoted by Don Conway-Long in "Working with Men Who Batter" (*Handbook of Counseling and Psychotherapy with Men*, Sage Publishing, 1987), p.306.

[3] Don Conway-Long, "Working with Men Who Batter (*Handbook of Counseling and Psychotherapy with Men*, Sage Publications, Murray Scher, Mark Stevens, Glen Good, and Gregg Eichenfield, eds., 1987), p.306.

[4] Friar Cherubino Siena, *Rules of Marriage*, quoted by Terry Davidson in *Conjugal Crime* (New York: Hawthorn Books, Inc., 1978), p.99.

[5] Michel Bograd, "Battered Wives and Co-Eds" (*Science News*, Vol. 124, September 17, 1983), p.187.

[6] Roger Langley and Richard C. Levy, *Wife-beating: The Silent Crisis* (New York: E.P. Dutton, 1977), p.81.

[7] John Greene, quoted in "Turbulent Teens: The Stress Factors" (*Psychology Today*, May, 1985), p.16.

[8] Diane Salvatore, "Teen Rage" (*Ladies Home Journal*, Vol. 104, February, 1987), p.96.

[9] Peter Merseburger, quoted by Rollo May in *Power and Innocence* (New York: W.W. Norton and Co., Inc., 1972), p.64.

[10] Claudette McShane, "Date Abuse: When Relationships Go Bad" (*Campus Life*, November, 1985), p.38.

[11] Fred Bruning, "A New Twist to Video Violence" (*Maclean's*, Vol. 100, June 8, 1987), p.9.

[12] Wendy Bowers, "Violent Pornography" (*Humanist*, Vol. 48, January/February, 1988), p.22.

[13] Bruning, p.9.

[14] Jean Doss, Community Outreach Coordinator, Committee to Aid Abused Women, Sparks NV, July 1985.

[15] Langley and Levy, p.52.

[16] Marie Winn, *Children Without Childhood* (New York: Pantheon Books, 1983), p.55.

[17] David Elkind, "Coping with Stress" (*Parents*, vol. 62, August, 1987). p.202.

[18] Winn, p.135.

Chapter 5
[1] Lenore Walker, *The Battered Woman*, (New York: Harper and Row, 1979), p.26.

[2] Elizabeth Fisher, *The Men In Our Lives*, (New York: William Morrow and Co., Inc., 1985), p.267.

[3] *Ibid.*, p.58.

[4] Susan Zakin, "Young Love, Violent Love," (*San Francisco Chronicle*, January 14, 1986).

[5] Roger Langley and Richard C. Levy, *Wife-Beating: The Silent Crisis*, (New York: E.P. Dutton, 1977), p.7.

[6] Shirley Rogers Radl. *The Invisible Woman*, (New York: Delacorte Press, 1983), p.70.

[7] Langley and Levy, p.112.

[8] Radl, p.17.

Chapter 6

[1] Don Conway-Long, Changing Men, St. Louis, Missouri, June 29, 1988.

[2] Alice Walker, quoted by Elizabeth Fishel in *The Men in Our Lives* (New York: William Morrow and Co., Inc., 1985), p.278.

[3] Andrea Sach, "Swinging—and Ducking—Singles" (*Time*, Sept. 5, 1988), p.54.

[4] Helen Benedict, *Safe, Strong, and Streetwise* (Boston: Little, Brown, and Co., 1987), p.51.

[5] Jim Long, "Date Abuse: When Relationships Go Bad" (*Campus Life*, November 1985), p.39.

[6] Benedict, p.51.

Chapter 7

[1] Helen Benedict, *Safe, Strong, and Streetwise* (Boston: Little, Brown and Co., 1987), p.51.

[2] Elizabeth Rodgers, "Sex and Your Body: Date Rape" (*Seventeen*, March, 1983), p.36.

[3] Leslie Cantrell, *Into the Light* (Edmonds, WA: Chas. Franklin Press, 1986), p.47.

[4] Susan Zakin, "Young Love, Violent Love," (San Francisco *Chronicle*, January 14, 1986), p.19.

[5] Abigail Van Buren, "Dear Abby" (Reno *Gazette-Journal*,

June 9, 1986).

[6] Zakin, p.19.

[7] *Ibid.*

[8] Rosemarie Bogal-Allbritten and William Allbritten, "Availability of Community Services to Student Victims of Courtship Violence," (*Response*, Vol. 10, No. 2, 1987), p.22.

[9] Jim Long, "Love Can Fool You" (*Campus Life*, February, 1986), p.29.

[10] Esther Lee Olson, *No Place to Hide* (Wheaton: Tyndale House Publishers, Inc., 1985), p.119.

[11] Benedict, p.151.

[12] Zakin, p.20.

[13] Susan Squire, "Are You Lost in Love?" (*Seventeen*, October 1985), p.197.

[14] quoted from an anonymous source by Cantrell, title page.

Chapter 8

[1] Don Conway-Long, "Working with Men Who Batter" (*Handbook of Counseling and Psychotherapy with Men*, Sage Publications, 1987, Murray Scher, Mark Stevens, Glen Good, and Gregg Eichenfield, eds.), p.305.

[2] Lenore Walker, reprinted in "Men, Women, and Violence" (*Raven*, St. Louis, MO).

[3] Ari Kiev, *Riding Through the Downers, Hassles, Snags, ,nd Funks* (New York: E.P. Dutton, 1980), p.65.

[4] David Seabury, *The Art of Selfishness* (New York: Julian Messner, 1964), p.237.

[5] "No Means No But" (*Emerge*, Cambridge, MA).

[6] Terry Davidson, Conjugal Crime, (New York, Hawthorn Books, Inc., 1978), p.155.

Chapter 9

[1] Nancy Rue, *Stop in the Name of Love* (New York: Rosen Publishing Group, 1988), p.103.

[2] *Ibid.*, pp.82–83.

Chapter 10

[1] Don Conway-Long, "Working with Men Who Batter," (*Handbook of Counseling and Psychotherapy with Men*, Sage Publications, Murray Scher et al., eds., 1987), p.318.

[2] Jim Long, "Date Abuse: When Relationships Go Bad" (*Campus Life*, November 1985), p.39.

[3] David Seabury, *The Art of Selfishness* (New York: Julian Messner, 1964), p.94.

[4] Barrie Levy, *Skills for Violence-free Relationships* (Southern California Coalition on Battered Women, 1984), p.59.

[5] *Ibid.*, p.50.

[6] Jim Long, quoted by Gregg Lewis in "Sometimes Girls Feel Weak" (*Campus Life*, January, 1986), p.63.

[7] Levy, p.51.

[8] Enid Lloyd Keljik, quoted by Terry Davidson in *Conjugal Crime* (New York: Hawthorn Books, Inc., 1978), p.94.

Bibliography

"Battered Wives and Co-Eds." *Science News*, Vol 124, September 17, 1983, p.187.

Benedict, Helen. *Safe, Strong, and Streetwise.* Boston: Little, Brown and Co., 1987.

Bogal-Allbritten, Rosemarie, and Allbritten, William. "Availability of Community Services to Student Victims of Courtship Violence." *Response*, Vol. 10, No. 2, 1987.

Bowers, Wendy. "Violent Pornography." *Humanist*, Vol. 48, January/February 1988, pp. 22–23, 42.

"Brawl in the Family." *Science News*, May 5, 1984, p.287.

Bruning, Fred. "A New Twist to Video Violence." *Maclean's*, Vol. 100, June 8, 1987, p.9.

Burkhart, Kathryn Watterson. *Growing into Love.* New York: G.P. Putnam's Sons, 1981.

Cantrell, Leslie. *Into the Light.* Edmunds, WA: Chas. Franklin Press, 7821 175th Street SW, 1986.

Chricton, Sara. "Dating Violence." *Seventeen*, August, 1982.

Conway-Long, Don. Changing Men. St. Louis, MO. June 29, 1988.

Conway-Long, Don. "Working with Men Who Batter." *Handbook of Counseling and Psychotherapy with Men.* Sage Publications. Scher, Stevens, Good, and Eichenfield, eds., 1987.

"Date Violence and Date Rape: Recognizing and Responding to the Early Warning Signs." *Emerge* Dating Violence Intervention Project, Cambridge, MA, 1988.

"Dating Violence Can Break More Than Your Heart." Michigan Coalition Against Domestic Violence, 1988.

Davidson, Terry. *Conjugal Crime*. New York: Hawthorn Books, Inc., 1978.

"Do You Act Like a Fool in Love?" *Seventeen*, June 1985, p.166.

Dobson, Dr. James. *Dare to Discipline*. New York: Bantam Books, 1970.

Dyer, Joyce. "Big Boys Don't Cry—But Why Not?" *Seventeen*, Vol. 46, March, 1987, pp.56–57, 295.

Elkind, David. "Coping with Stress." *Parents*, Vol. 62, August, 1987, p.202.

Englund, Steven. *Manslaughter*. Garden City: Doubleday and Company, Inc., 1983.

Fields, Suzanne. *Like Father, Like Daughter*. Boston: Little, Brown and Co., 1983.

Fishel, Elizabeth. *The Men in Our Lives*. New York: William Morrow and Co., Inc., 1985.

Goodman, Susan. "The Fine Art of Taking Control of Your Life." *Current Health*, Vol. 13, January 1987.

Helgesen, Sally. "Your Right to Say No." *Seventeen*, August, 1981.

Kiev, Ari. *Riding Through the Downers, Hassles, Snags, and Funks*. New York: E.P. Dutton, 1980.

Langley, Roger, and Levy, Richard C. *Wife-Beating: The Silent Crisis*. New York: E.P. Dutton, 1977.

Levy, Barrie. "Dating Violence." Southern California Coalition on Battered Women, Vol. VIII, No. 3, July, 1983.

Levy, Barrie. *Skills For Violence-Free Relationships*. Southern California Coalition on Battered Women, 1984.

Lewis, Gregg. "Sometimes Girls Feel Weak." *Campus Life*, January 1986, pp.58–63.

Long, Jim, et al. "Date Rape." *Campus Life*, December 1985, pp.42–47.

Long, Jim, et al. "Love Can Fool You." *Campus Life*, February, 1986, pp.26–31.

May, Rollo. *Power and Innocence*. New York: W.W. Norton & Co., Inc., 1972.

McCoy, Kathy. "What Do You Owe a Steady Boyfriend?" *Seventeen*, June, 1983, pp.34–36.

McShane, Claudette. "Date Abuse: When Relationships Go Bad." *Campus Life*, November 1985, pp.35–38.

"Men, Women and Violence." Raven Counseling Resources for Men, 1988.

NiCarthy, Ginny. *Getting Free: A Handbook for Women in Abusive Relationships*. Seattle: Seal Press, 1982.

Olson, Esther Lee. *No Place to Hide*, Wheaton: Tyndale House Publishers, Inc., 1985.

Peele, Stanton. *Love and Addiction*. New York: Taplinger Publishing Co., 1975.

Radl, Shirley Rogers. *The Invisible Woman*. New York: Delacorte Press, 1983.

"Respect...It Goes a Long Way." *Emerge* Dating Violence Intervention Project, Cambridge, MA, 1988.

Rodgers, Elizabeth. "Sex and Your Body: Date Rape." *Seventeen*, March, 1983, pp.36, 40.

Sachs, Andrea. "Swinging—and Ducking—Singles." *Time*, September 5, 1988, p.54.

Safran, Claire. "Why Men Hurt the Women They Love." *Reader's Digest*, January 1986.

Salvatore, Diane. "Teen Rage." *Ladies Home Journal*, Vol. 104, February, 1987, pp.95–97, 154–156.

Seabury, David. *The Art of Selfishness*. New York: Julian Messner, 1964.

Shorris, Earl. "Reflections on Power." *Harper's Bazaar*, July, 1985, pp.51–54.

Sisk, John P. "Our Savage Spectacles." *Harper's Bazaar*, July, 1985, pp.64–68.

Sonkin, Daniel Jay, and Durphy, Michael. *Learning to Live Without Violence*. San Francisco: Volcano Press, 1982.

Sousa, Carol. *Emerge*, Cambridge, MA. August 9, 1988.

Spock, Benjamin. "How On-Screen Violence Hurts Your Kids." *Redbook*, Vol. 170, November, 1987, pp.26–28.

Squire, Susan. "Are You Lost in Love?" *Seventeen*, October, 1985.

Stacey, William A., and Shupe, Anson. *The Family Secret*. Boston: Beacon Press, 1983.

"The Dark Side of Love." *People Weekly*, Vol. 28, October 26, 1987, pp.88–98.

"The Unhappy Years." *Scientific American*, Vol. 256, January 1987, p.60.

Toch, Hans. *Violent Men*. Chicago: Aldine Publishing Co., 1969.

"Tough Times for Teens." *USA today*, Vol. 116, September 1987, pp.9–10.

"Trouble in the Family." *Life*, March 1982, pp.72–80.

"Turbulent Teens: The Stress Factors." *Psychology Today*, May, 1985, p.15.

VanBuren, Abigail. "Dear Abby." Reno *Gazette-Journal*, June 9, 1986.

Walker, Lenore E. *The Battered Woman*. New York: Harper and Row, 1979.

Walters, Barbara, and Glass, Ellen. "Eight Great Anger-Busters." *Seventeen*, Vol. 46, pp.80, 304.

Winn, Marie. *Children Without Childhood*. New York: Pantheon Books, 1983.

Zakin, Susan. "Young Love, Violent Love." San Francisco *Chronicle*, January 14, 1986.

Index

isolation
of abuser, 94, 95
of victim, 10, 21, 22, 46, 81

J
jealousy
of family/friends, 18, 57
of victim, 3, 10, 11, 17, 23, 31,
46, 64, 69, 70, 71, 72, 98, 103

K
Keljik, Enid Lloyd, 124
Koval, James, 14

L
limits, setting sexual, 74
loneliness
of abuser, 94
teenage, 4
Long, Jim, 74, 87, 118, 123

M
machismo image, 44, 56, 64, 67,
122
manipulation, 22, 26, 94
marriage skills, learning, 10, 12
masculinity, mistaken beliefs
about, 39–40, 42–43
McShane, Claudette, 9, 12
media, and violence, 48–50,
115, 123
Men in Our Lives, The, 55–56
mental illness, 37, 40, 91
Morrell, Lisa, 9
movies, 63
slice-and-dice, 48, 123
music videos, violence on,
48–49, 63, 123
myths, destroying, 29–38, 58,
110, 113

N
name-calling, 7, 12, 18, 21, 47,
68, 78, 97
National Council Against
Domestic Violence, 94–95
needs

denial of, 21
expressing, 100
satisfying, 13, 65–66, 72, 99
negotiation strategy, 121
Norman, Jane, 62
no, saying, 25, 35–36, 49–50,
72, 74–75, 102–103

O
obscenity, 21, 22, 41, 47
overprotection, 52–53, 57, 84

P
parents
abuse by, 103
confiding in, 8, 83–84
making deal with, 74
violence between, 61, 103
Parnas, Raymond, 14
police, reporting to, 55, 111
pornography, 48–49, 68
possessions, destruction of, 18,
21, 22
possessiveness, 24, 31, 57, 69, 91
power
maintaining, 23–24, 41, 43,
44, 73
over others, 101
regaining, 51
strategy, 121
pressure, cracking under, 6, 30,
47
problem-solving, 121
promise, of reform, 5, 57, 79, 92
punishment, physical, 51–52
put-downs, 11, 18, 21, 67, 80,
98–99, 103, 104, 122

R
rage, venting, 4, 7, 36, 43, 45
rape, 10, 11, 26, 32, 45, 48, 55,
78, 83–84, 123
relationship
abusive, 10–11, 14–15,
16–17, 27, 54, 59
avoiding, 64–75
breakup of, 57, 81–86, 96, 111
confusion about, 27